MATTY
and the
MORON
and
MADONNA

I do not look away. The terrified people left to the dark are in the tenement of my own street.
DONALD ROY HORWITZ

Somewhere down a darkened hall the Moron tolls his awful bell.
H.L.

MATTY
and the
MORON
and
MADONNA

❧

A play by Herbert Lieberman

A *Spotlight Dramabook*

HILL AND WANG — NEW YORK

Gift - Wright Theatre 12/1987

FIRST PRINTING JANUARY 1964

Manufactured in the United States of America by
The Colonial Press Inc., Clinton, Massachusetts

For
Billy and Amy Rossman

ACKNOWLEDGMENTS

I would like to acknowledge my indebtedness to Dr. Martin Sulkow, who helped me to understand better the characters of this play, and to Miss Burry Frederik, who helped me to portray them.

H.L.

MATTY
and the
MORON
and
MADONNA

CHARACTERS

MATTY MOLLUSCA, *boy about nine years old*
DOMINICK MOLLUSCA, *Matty's father*
ROSE MOLLUSCA, *Matty's mother*
AUGIE HENSCHEL, *boy about thirteen years old*
MR. FINNERTY, *teacher*
ALEC CUSHMAN
GAIL
TWILIGHT } *Matty's classmates*
FIRST BOY
SECOND BOY
TOMMY CARBO, *bartender*
FIRST MAN
SECOND MAN
THIRD MAN
FOURTH MAN } *people in the bar*
FIFTH MAN
BEGGAR
RABBI LICHTER, *tenant of the building*
LILA RIKER, *Dominick's girlfriend*
MRS. CUSHMAN, *mother of Alec*
STELLA RIZZO, *tenant of the building*
VITO TUSSI, *Stella's boyfriend*
FACELESS, *tenant of the building*
MARIA ESPOSITO, *Madonna, tenant of the building*
JUAN ESPOSITO, *her son, the moron*

THE SETTING: The only set is a cutaway, designed beehive fashion to permit the audience to look into a number of cell-like apartments in a New York slum dwelling. There is an upper and lower level to the cutaway, with a hall staircase that permits people to move up and down freely between the floors. Each dwelling has only the most meager token furnishings—portable, and so arranged that each cell can be transformed quickly into another person's apartment in another part of the building. The saloon set for Act Two is located in the lower center part of the cutaway. However, when action is going on in one of the cell-like apartments, the others are blacked out, revealing only the motionless silhouettes—shadowy and scarcely perceptible—of actors waiting to go on.

The time is the present.

10

ACT ONE

SCENE I

A *poorly furnished boy's bedroom in what is obviously a tenement apartment. It is night and the moon streams through the naked glass of an uncurtained window. An old and rickety brass bed glows like the skeleton of a shipwreck in a shaft of moonlight. The bed is empty—its blankets and pillows thrown in a sort of careless disarray. Around the room are the symbols of boyhood—a battered kite, a sail-less sailboat, and other half-wrecked, half-patched paraphernalia. It is a warm, balmy night in May. The sky is full of electricity, and a peculiar silence dreams over the scene.*

A small boy of about nine years is silhouetted at the window. He is seated on the sill, wearing only the tops of his pajamas and a pair of Jockey shorts. He holds a magnifying glass up and gazes skyward through it. Offstage, there are the muffled voices of a man and a woman. Their words are fuzzy and incoherent as if they were being poured through the plaster walls. Their tone is full of menace and it is easy to guess that quite a row is being kicked up somewhere in a different room. The boy, however, appears to be oblivious of the sounds. Nothing disturbs his perusal of the heavens.

In the next moment, a hall door slams; the sudden and complete silence that follows seems to jolt the boy out of his stargazings. He springs into bed, covering himself and carefully tucking his magnifier under his pillow. He pretends to be asleep. The door to his room suddenly swings open and a woman, who may be described simply as drab and fattish, stands framed in the doorway. The moon seems to follow her as she walks in trancelike fashion across the room toward the boy's bed. She carries a hatchet by her side. She stops at the head of the bed and gazes down at the boy. Slowly she raises the hatchet and suddenly brings it down with the speed of a

11

guillotine. *The boy, who has been awake through all of this, manages to save his life by rolling out of the bed and onto the floor. The hatchet, having missed him by inches, gongs horribly on the brass head of the bed, near where, only moments before, the boy's head rested.*

The boy now lies on the floor, panting and staring up at his mother who gazes down upon him strangely. Neither can communicate with the other. It is suddenly evident that the woman is in a trance. She turns slowly and retraces her steps to the door. She still carries the hatchet. The boy lies on the floor, staring after her in a fit of trembling. The boy's heavy, broken breathing is still heard as the stage slowly blacks out.

SCENE II

The stage lights gradually transform the night of the previous scene into a slowly coming dawn, which is suggested by a green hue that hovers over the stage. The shadowy figure of a man is seen moving hurriedly through a kitchen. He gives the appearance of a robber as he rifles frantically through closets and drawers. Those items which he takes, he stuffs into an old Gladstone bag. His packing is done with bullishness and nervous haste. As he crosses the room, he stubs his toe and mutters fiercely beneath his breath, "Butan a la Madon——" and returns to his packing with more determination. Then he pulls out one drawer and turns its contents over onto the floor. Pasted to the underside of this drawer is an envelope. Ripping it open, he stuffs green bills into his pocket. As he does this, bills spill out and onto the floor. He bends to retrieve them and suddenly, in his stooped position, he sees a small phantasmal form in shirt and trousers. It is the boy of Scene I. He is barefoot. The man lurches backward in fright, stuffing all the money roughly out of sight and into his pocket. The man is DOMINICK Mol-lusca. *The boy is his son, Matthew Mollusca—*MATTY.

Dom. Jesus Christ. You gotta sneak around here like a ghost? [*Goes back to his packing even more furiously.*] How long you been standing there like that—spying on me? [*The boy remains silent.*] Put your slippers on.

Matty. Where you goin'? [*He holds the magnifier in his hand.*]

Dom. Put your slippers on, I told you.

Matty. Are you goin' somewhere?

Dom. I'm goin' on a big business trip—negotiatin' the sale of the Grand Coolie Dam to the Russian government. [*He continues to pack hastily.*]

Matty [*wide-eyed*]. Really?

Dom [*stopped by the boy's naïveté*]. No, kiddo—not really. Hand me them shorties.

Matty [*helping his father*]. You goin' far away?

Dom. If I could get me on one them moon flights, I'd take it—monkeys and all.

Matty. Where you goin'?

Dom. Anywhere away from your mother—where I can breathe. Now you and her can have each other all to yourselves—real cozy—like you always wanted.

Matty. You ever——

Dom. Quit it, will ya. Go look at somethin' through that glass of yours. Stella ought to be droppin' her nightie by this time.

Matty. You ever comin' home again?

Dom [*looks up from his packing*]. Would you care? [*The boy's silence is painful for the father. Suddenly the tinkling of bells is heard from somewhere beneath them. They have the sound of sleigh bells at Christmastime.*] The bells of St. Iddy.

Matty. It's a sin to call him St. Iddy. His name's Juan.

The bells continue to tinkle.

Dom. So why don't he act like a Juan instead of an Iddy —ding-dong-dingin' down there all day like an idiot.

Matty. That's how he says good mornin'.

Dom. That's why I call him Iddy. You seen my socks?

Matty. Nope.

Dom [*rummages about*]. What about the ones you're sittin' on? [*He pulls socks from under* MATTY.]

Matty. He's learnin' to eat with a knife and fork.

Dom. That ain't no big deal at nineteen. Hand me them ties.

Matty [*handing ties to* DOM]. He——

Dom. He, he, he. A million kids on the block and you gotta go latch on to a Spick Mongolian.

Matty. What's that?

Dom. A Mongolian? Oh, that's some kinda Asiatic fever they got over in Mongolia.

Matty. How could Juan catch that if he never been to Mongolia?

Dom. How come every time I answer one question, you got three more?

Matty. Madonna says——

Dom. *Butana Madonna.*

Matty. What?

Dom. I said hand me that brush over there. [MATTY *reaches over to hand a hairbrush to* DOM, *but it falls noisily to the floor.*] Jesus Christ! Now you done it. She'll be out here and squawkin' in a minute.

He tosses articles into the Gladstone and starts to wrestle its brimming contents closed.

Matty [*coming forward*]. I'll help.

Dom. Just sit there.

MATTY *returns to the chair. He sits silently while* DOM *wrestles with the Gladstone.*

Matty. Madonna has a real church window in her living room—with all kinds of different colors and a picture of the Holy Mother in it. And it came all the way across the ocean from Barcelona, Spain.

Dom. All the way across the Hudson River from Paterson, New Jersey, is more like it.

Matty. Whenever you want somethin' from the Holy Mother, all you gotta do is kneel down in front of her—like this— [*Kneeling and clasping his hands.*] and say "Hail

Mary, full of grace. Hail Mary, full of grace," and she'll answer you.

Dom. Yeah? Don't hold your breath waitin'.

Matty. It's true.

Dom. Get off your knees. [MATTY *rises.*] I suppose Madonna told you that. I'll tell you somethin' about that Madonna of yours. Your buddy wouldn't be in the shape he's in today if she wasn't such a *butan.* [*Suddenly catches sight of something and peers eagerly out of the window.*] Hey, hand me that glass of yours for a second, will ya? [MATTY *gives the magnifier to his father who peers through it clownishly.*] Hey, come here. [MATTY *backs away.*] Come here, I said.

Matty. Mama says it's a sin to look at naked women.

Dom. What your mama really meant was that some dames are in such bad shape that it's a sin to have to look at 'em naked. [*Looking through the glass again.*] That's a blessing up there.

Matty. Mama says——

Dom [*turning angrily*]. And your papa says it's no sin. How come you always take her word?

Matty. 'Cause she's always right.

Dom. Who told your mama it's a sin?

Matty. Grandmother.

Dom. Your grandma was a bigger nut than your mother even. [*Slips off his outer garments.*]

Matty. You shouldn't talk that way about someone sick.

Dom. Sick—my aspidistras.

Matty. She's got cancer of the face.

Dom. Pimples ain't cancer. Cancer ain't pimples. Just 'cause someone in your family dies of cancer don't mean you automatically gotta go the same way.

Matty. Mama says——

Dom. Your mama'll outlive me and you. Now I don't wanna hear no more about what she says——

Suddenly *a scratching sound is heard on the door.*

Matty. It's Liddle.

Dom. Go get him—quick, before he breaks down the door and has her up and howling.

MATTY *goes off.* DOM *starts hastily putting on a clean shirt and suit.* MATTY *returns, carrying an alley cat in his arms.*

Matty. His ear's bleeding. Bet it was the dirty old tomcat lives down the cellar.

Dom [*examining the cat's ear*]. If it was, he used a penknife.

Matty. What? [DOM *pours milk in a saucer for the cat.*] Just lemme see that ol' cat again.

Dom [*starting to dress again*]. You really wanna know where I'm goin', kid? Out west.

Matty [*excitedly*]. Really?

Dom [*putting his finger over his mouth*]. Sh—sh——. Yeah. Really.

Matty. Where in the west?

Dom. Wyoming, Utah, Colorado. The whole damn territory if I please.

Matty. Are you gonna be a cowboy?

Dom. Why not? Join up with a ranch, wrangle for a while. Then maybe even get a spread of my own, and I'll never fix another john or sink or busted main. I'll hire plumbers myself and just supervise. [*He suddenly realizes that the boy is trembling.*] Hey! Whatsa matter with you?

Matty [*turning away*]. Nothin'.

Dom. Nothin'? You're shakin' like a leaf. What's wrong?

Matty. I had a bad dream.

Dom. So what. I get 'em all the time—even when I'm awake. What was it?

Matty. I don't hardly remember. I was in a place that was empty—just sky and air—and snow fallin'——

Dom. So far I ain't scared.

Matty. And I was runnin' away from someone who was chasing me.

Dom. Who?

Matty. Faceless. It was Faceless. He wanted to catch me and kill me.

Dom. You mean the poor cripple guy lives down the third floor?

Matty. He's killed lots of kids.

Dom [impatiently]. Come on——

Matty. He goes out nights looking for kids—and if he catches one, he makes him look at his face—and then he cuts him up in a million little pieces——

Dom. For Chrissake. Where do you get them fairy tales?

Matty. It's true.

Dom. Yeah, sure. [*He buckles his belt hurriedly.*] I gotta beat it before she's up.

Matty [clutching his heart]. Somethin' hurts my heart.

Dom. Nothin' hurts your heart. You're just a little scared 'cause I'm goin'. Quit shakin'!

Matty. I can't help it.

Dom. Neither can I, kiddo. Some day you'll understand that. [DOM *turns to the mirror and starts to knot his tie.*] If she gets real bad—I mean if she tries anything funny— phone the police. Don't go to them direct. Call 'em and tell 'em what's happenin'—then beat it. Run away—work on a farm, be a bum, be anything, but don't be a ward of the state.

Matty. You took all our money.

Dom. What d'ya mean?

Matty. I saw you from the door.

Dom. Oh, that. I was meanin' to give it to you. Glad you reminded me. [*He takes some bills out and stuffs them in* MATTY's *pocket.*] Here's twenty. It's your ol' man's legacy. Four bits for every year of his life. Don't let your mama swipe it on you. [*He reaches down and lifts the bag.*] Wanna come? [MATTY *is silent.*] We stand a better chance if we stick together. [*He looks at the boy urgently, but* MATTY *looks out the window through the magnifier.* DOM *laughs, though he is plainly hurt.*] We're not so wild about each other, are we, kiddo? You're your mama's boy—a regular little saint. [*The sound of bells tinkles up from below. Suddenly* DOM *kneels down to* MATTY.] Hey—just once—before I go—call me Papa. [MATTY *remains silent as* DOM *kneels awkwardly. Finally* Dom *stands and snatches his raincoat cheerily.*] It's gonna be hot as hell today. Grow good kid. [Dom *starts to leave, when suddenly a high, sweet humming is heard from the next room. He bolts to the outer door, opens it, and pauses on the threshold. Both father and son stand riveted to the floor, staring at each other, as the high, sweet humming drifts into the room. A determined expression crosses* Dom's *face as he looks at* Matty. Dom *speaks in a harsh, urgent whisper.*] Matty. [*The boy stares silently at his father, then backs slowly toward the humming.* Dom *smiles.*] She sure can sing pretty, your ma. [*He leaves.*]

Matty *is now alone. Suddenly the bells tinkle from below.* Matty *runs to the window, opens it, and calls down.*

Matty. Good morning, Juan. Good morning, Madonna.

Madonna [*from offstage*]. Buenas dias, Angelito.

There is some laughter and chatter, and then suddenly Matty *ducks his head back into the room. From out on the window ledge, he has brought in the hatchet that was nearly the instrument of his execution. He looks impassively at it for a while. Then he starts to swing it through the air in a childlike way, inscribing wide, whooshing arcs. He emits a short Indian war cry and laughs at his own nonsense. Then, in the next moment, the boy gently runs the sharp edge of the hatchet across his throat.* Matty *does this in a profoundly serious way as if he were cautiously becoming the friend of a dangerous person. The humming is heard again from the next room. At the sound,* Matty *runs to the window, replaces the hatchet on the ledge, and goes to the table and pours a saucer of milk for the cat. He sits down at the table and calls.*

Matty. Here, Liddle. Here, Little, Liddle.

The door behind Matty *opens and we see the woman of the first scene. She is a shade under what would be called fat. The face is almost naked of expression, the head covered with a mat of dull, lifeless blond hair that looks like a doll's wig. She stands regarding the boy from the doorway. He is unaware of her presence. He calls his cat and talks to it.*

There is a distant, enigmatic expression on her face as she starts to tiptoe across the room toward the boy.

Matty. Come on out, Liddle. Don't be scared. I won't let that old tomcat hurt you. He picks on you 'cause he knows you don't have no mama. [*The* MOTHER *stops behind the boy's chair and stares down at him.*] I'll look after you, Liddle. I'll protect you.

Slowly the MOTHER *raises her arms and then gently covers the boy's eyes with her hands.* MATTY *starts up, but in the next instant he is reassured by the high, soft, almost musical laughter of the* MOTHER.

Mother. Guess.

Matty [*laughing*]. I don't know.

Mother. Guess anyway.

Matty. I can't.

Mother. Then you have to pay the consequences. [*She hugs him till he gasps for breath. They laugh happily.*] Matty, Matty, scaredy-catty. You jumped like a puppet on a string. Like that——

She imitates a puppet's jerky mechanical motions. MATTY *claps and laughs in delight.*

Matty. I did not.

Mother. You did.

Matty. I did not, I did not. I wasn't scared a bit.

Mother [*coming upon him and embracing him*]. Give your mother a kiss, Starfish.

Matty [*embracing her warmly*]. How come you call me "Starfish"?

Mother. 'Cause you have five arms to hug me. [*She laughs and hugs him.*] Don't you like that name? I'll give you another. [*Thinks a moment.*] What about—"Cockroach"?

Matty. What about "Elephant"?

Mother. "Beetle"?

Matty. What about "Giraffe"—or "Kangaroo"?

Mother. What about "Spider"?

Matty. I guess—— I'll be "Starfish."

Mother [*picking up the milk bottle from the table*]. What happened to the milk?

Matty. I gave it to Liddle. He cut his ear scrapin' with the tomcat.

Mother. You can't run off to school without milk.

Matty. It's all right.

Mother. Stop off at the candy store and have a glass before you go into school, hear?

Matty [*happily*]. O.K. O.K.

Mother. Was that your father's voice I heard out here a few minutes ago?

Matty [*uncomfortably*]. Yes. He's gone.

Mother. I know. I sent him away.

Matty. He's gone out west.

Mother. Where out west?

Matty. A whole lot of places, he said. He asked me to go with him.

The MOTHER *goes hastily to the closet where a young boy's suit,* MATTY's *suit, is hanging. She throws it roughly into the center of the room.*

Mother. Go ahead.

Matty. I don't wanna go. I wanna stay with you.

He goes to pick up his suit and the MOTHER *comes quickly to him. She kneels beside him and hugs him desperately.*

Mother. We'll be happy, love. [*She takes the suit and folds it neatly, placing it on a chair.*] He wouldn't have taken you, anyway. He doesn't care a hoot for you. You know that, don't you?

Matty. Yes.

Mother. Tell me what else he said.

Matty [*animatedly*]. He said he was gonna be a cowboy.

Mother. A cowboy? [*She bursts into laughter.*] Oh, Dominick, Dominick. Won't you ever grow up? [*To* MATTY.] Are you sorry he's gone?

Matty. No. I'm happy.

Mother. Well, then, try and look that way. He would have ruined our lives. He would've pulled us down. So I got rid of him. I had to. I had no choice. [*She kneels again before him.*] He wanted to separate us.

Matty. I know.

Mother. Well, he failed. And we're still together. So cheer up, love. We're going to be fine. [*She hugs him and tickles him and he squirms with delight. Suddenly she notices* MATTY's *shirt.*] You can't wear that shirt to school. It's filthy.

Matty. I just put it on yesterday.

Mother. Put on a fresh white one—and a tie.

Matty. No one else in the class wears a tie. Why do I have to?

Mother. Because you're mine—that's why. So that teacher'll see you and know right off you're the smartest.

Matty. I'm not the smartest.

Mother [*aggressively*]. Who's smarter?

Matty. Mr. Finnerty says Alec is the smartest.

Mother. Mr. Finnerty is a fool. Anyone with half an eye could see that Alec Cushman can't hold a candle to you when it comes to intellect. You're the smartest. [MATTY *stares at her uncertainly.*] Say it. Say you're the smartest.

Matty. I'm—— I'm the smartest.

Mother. Don't hesitate. Say it right off. "I'm the smartest, I'm the smartest." And it'll be true. Say it.

Matty. I'm the smartest.

The MOTHER *stands in front of the mirror. Looking at herself, she runs her fingers lightly over her face.*

Mother. Look. Here's a new one. Want to feel it? [MATTY *goes to her, and she takes his hand and runs it over her face.*] Like tiny red rubies. Hard and bright and red. How fast it's spreading through me.

Matty [*frightened*]. No, Mama.

Mother. It's you who'll suffer when I'm gone.

Matty. Please don't say that, Mama. It scares me.

Mother. Don't be afraid. I promise I won't leave you alone to— [*Indicating apartment.*] this.

Matty. We'll go to Borella. He'll be able to help you.

Mother. No one can help me any more. It's too far along. Soon I'll be——

Matty [*crying out*]. Mama!

Mother [*hugging him*]. I didn't mean that, love. I'll get better. I'll get well. [*Suddenly noticing his hair.*] Look at your hair. Growing right down your neck.

She goes to a drawer and takes out a pair of scissors. Then she takes MATTY *onto her lap and starts to trim his hair. His face reveals his great uneasiness.*

Matty. This morning he tried to get me to look at Stella Rizzo—undressed. But I wouldn't do it.

Mother [*trimming* MATTY's *hair*]. Don't judge him harshly, love. He's an uneducated man. He don't know any better.

Matty. I hope he never comes back.

Mother. You never really knew your father. If you'd known him twenty years ago, you might have felt differently about him today. First time I ever laid eyes on him was at the state fair outside of Muncie. I was seventeen. I remember walking with your grandmother from exhibit to exhibit and then coming to a great crowd that was gathered around one of the events. Right in the center of that crowd was your father, swinging one of those hammers they give you and you have to ring the bell to measure how strong you are. He had his shirt and jacket off. Bare to the chest. It took my breath away. [*She laughs girlishly.*] He rang the bell twenty-two times that afternoon. I wanted to stay around and watch him some more, but your grandmother got furious with me—made me go on to the jam-tasting. He had the makings of a grand man, your father. Handsome—powerful —and shy and gentle. I married him against my mother's wishes—and that was the only time I ever let my feelings get the better of my good judgment. I paid dearly for that mistake. Learn a lesson from me, love. Don't ever disobey your mother, hear? [MATTY *nods yes, and she resumes clipping his hair.*] Did your grandmother try and hurt you again last night?

Matty [*almost whispering*]. Yes.

Mother. Don't worry. I won't let her. As long as I'm here, she can't hurt you.

Matty. Am I going to die?

Mother. Not for a long long time, dear.

Matty. I don't want to—ever.

Mother. I won't let you. I'll protect you.

Matty. I always try to be good.

Mother. You'll go to heaven, love.

Matty. I wanna meet the Heavenly Father.

Mother. You will, love, you will. Now off to school. [*She lifts him from her lap.*]

Matty. Lemme stay home today.

Mother. That's not my idea of being good.

Matty. But I don't wanna leave you.

Mother. Please go, love.

Matty. You won't be here when I get back.

Mother [*backing away from* MATTY]. Please go.

Matty. We can go up on the roof and play "Starfish." [*He hugs her around the legs and starts to sing.*]

"Starfish, Starfish, huggin' to a rock

'Long came a typhoon and flipped him up the dock——"

Mother. You're choking me to death.

Matty. I ain't goin'.

Mother [*slaps him viciously across the face*]. Say it again and see what you get.

Matty. I didn't mean it! I didn't mean it!

Mother. Commonness. That's your father's work. Say it correct. [*Shakes him.*] You say it correct or I'll split your head.

Matty [*trembling, slowly and deliberately with his eyes closed*]. I'm not goin'.

Mother. That's better. Don't you ever open a gutter mouth to me again. Now get ready for school. [MATTY *starts slowly to put on a sweater. She approaches him regretfully and puts some coins in his pocket.*] Money for lunch.

Matty. Will you be here when I come home?

Mother. Yes.

Matty. You promise?

Mother. Yes. And maybe I'll make ginger candy while you're at school.

Matty [*excitedly*]. And play "Starfish"?

Mother. Yes. But don't wear that sweater today. Wear the red.

Matty. The red itches.

Mother [*flares*]. Wear the red, I said. [*Smothering her rage.*] Please make me happy, love. I'm feeling so sad.

Matty [*changing*]. O.K.

Mother. And today—in front of Mr. Finnerty, you show up Alec Cushman.

Matty. All right, Mama.

He is happy. He picks up his books and starts to go.

Mother [*calling to him*]. Don't worry, love. I'll get better. You'll see. We're gonna be fine. [MATTY *now opens the door and she runs to hug him.*] I'm sorry I hit you, love.

MATTY *kisses her hand for a long moment and then turns away, whistling happily.*

SCENE III

MATTY *skips out of the door as if nothing unusual had happened to him in the last few hours. He starts to bound down the rickety hall when he comes to a screeching halt before the black leather figure of a young tough who blocks the stairway. This is* AUGIE HENSCHEL, *the building bully.*

AUGIE. You're gonna break your neck, chicken.

Matty. I'm late for school.

Augie. You stepped on my shoe.

Matty. I'm sorry, Augie.

MATTY *tries to get past him but is blocked.*

Augie. You ain't apologized for steppin' on my shoes yet. Well, I'm gonna let you make it up to me.

AUGIE *starts to drag* MATTY *down the steps.*

Matty [*resisting*]. I don't wanna go down the cellar.

Augie. I gotta initiate you into the Crate Club.

Matty. I don't wanna join.

Augie. That ain't the way you talked Friday afternoon.

Matty. I only watched. I never did a thing.

Augie [*laughing*]. You lyin' bastard.

Matty [*protesting*]. I only watched. It was you and Frankie and Lenny Morello.

He attempts to get by AUGIE *again and is roughly blocked.*

Augie. What makes you think you're so special?

Matty. I gotta go. I'm gonna be late.

Augie. If you wanna go, fight me. [MATTY *stands unmoving.*] Come on and fight. [MATTY *remains silent and passive.*] My brother told me Madonna's a whoo-a. [*Watching* MATTY *for a reaction.*] She sells it. You know what else he told me? He told me your ol' lady's out of her skull. [MATTY *is still passively silent.*] If someone said that about my ol' lady, I'd skull 'em, and I can't stand my ol' lady. [MATTY *remains silent with lowered head.*] I never seen anybody who could lay back and take a beating faster than you. [*He suddenly seizes* MATTY *and applies a cruel half nelson.*] Why'nt you ever fight back, for Chrissake?

Matty [*not even struggling*]. I know you'd whip me.

Augie. That ain't no reason. [*Grips harder.*] Gimme a nickel. [MATTY *is silent.*] I said—gimme a nickel.

Matty. If I give you one, will you lemme go?

Augie. Soon as you show me the nickel.

Matty. You promise?

Augie. Sure. I promise.

MATTY *goes through his pockets, comes up with the quarter his mother gave him, and gives it to* AUGIE, *who snatches it and pockets it.*

Matty. Hey, that was a quarter.

Augie. So it was.

Matty. So I get twenty cents back.

Augie. I'll take it and open up a bank account for you.

Matty. You promised.

Augie. I never promise. It's un-American.

Matty. That's my lunch money.

Augie. I gotta eat too, chicken. And I figure it comes out to just the price of the lesson I taught you.

Matty. What lesson?

Augie. Livin' is takin'. Now beat it, chicken—and if you open your trap to your ol' lady, I'll break your fingers. [*He shoves* MATTY *down the remaining stairs and tosses his books after him.*] You're goin' down that cellar one of these days, chicken. You better believe it.

AUGIE *goes off singing.* MATTY *picks himself up. Then he picks up his scattered books and goes slowly down the steps. At the foot of the steps he knocks on the door of an apartment.*

Matty. Madonna—Madonna. [*No answer.*] Madonna.

MATTY *knocks again and listens. Finally he goes down the stairs and out.*

SCENE IV

Back in the Mollusca apartment, the MOTHER *is walking about, picking up items and straightening things. Discovering one of* MATTY's *suits on the chair where she had placed it, she picks it up and tenderly puts it on a hanger, embracing the suit as if the child were still in it. She hangs it on the closet door. Gradually the stage becomes darker and gloomier. Thunder is heard. The* MOTHER *drifts to the stove and sets a teakettle boiling. A clock ticks, and the sound of a hurdy-gurdy floats up from below. The woman now stands before the mirror, gazing hypnotically at her image. A great clap of thunder and, in the next instant, a weird atonal music are heard. The music is suggestive of the woozy, dreamy disorientation of psychotic states. The kettle on the*

*stove starts its high shrill whistle, and the sound of the
ticking clock and the hurdy-gurdy mount to a frightening
volume, as suddenly Mrs. Mollusca and her side of the stage
are completely blacked out.*

*Light falls on two masked female characters locked in a long
embrace. This takes place behind a diaphanous curtain that
is blown gently by a fan to produce a dreamlike underwater
illusion. One of the figures is dressed in a flowing red gown.
She is tall and on stilts to increase her height. The other
figure is short and round, almost mummylike, in a tightly
confining white garment. The dance that we see is built
upon the embrace. The smaller figure in white is clearly a
love captive to the taller woman in red. The shadow of a
huge spider is projected behind the dancers. The movements
of this spider entice the small figure in white who breaks
away from her love captor in red and flies to the spider
shadow that gradually envelops her. As this occurs, the
figure of the woman in white goes red under a crimson light.
At this moment, the red figure on stilts points accusingly at
the figure beneath the spider's shadow—and then crumbles
in a mass of red gauze on the floor. The new figure in red is
now completely swallowed in the spider's tentacles.*

*In the next moment, the side of the stage in which Mrs.
Mollusca was standing is lit again. The* MOTHER *still stands
transfixed before the mirror as the teakettle, the clock, and
the hurdy-gurdy all drift in on her once more. She starts to
walk slowly, somnambulistically, across the stage as all the
sounds in the room become magnified. She moves to the
boy's suit, which she hung on the door a little earlier. She
picks up the pair of scissors, and she stops before the little
suit. Slowly raising the shears, she proceeds to slash the
garment. First she slashes slowly, a soft, tender moaning rising from her throat. The strokes grow more and more furious
as the sound in her throat turns to a horrible gurgle. Now
she stabs the suit repeatedly with short, frenzied jabs as the
stage blacks out.*

SCENE V

*The stage is in darkness except for a circle of light in which
five or six children are seated. The arrangement of the children should suggest a classroom. A man stands before the
group. All the children raise their hands frantically toward
the* TEACHER, *except for* MATTY, *who sits alone toward the
rear.*

ALEC. Me—me—Mr. Finnerty.

Teacher. Alec.

Alec [a bright-looking child of nine or ten]. 1212 anno
Domini.

Teacher. Correct. And what happened in this year? Gail?

Gail [a young girl rises]. The shepherd Stephen came to
Philip Augustus and told him that Christ appeared to him
while he was tending his flock and told him to lead a Children's Crusade to the Holy Land.

Teacher. What did Philip think of that?

Twilight [a bright young Negro boy]. He thought Stephen
was a little kooked and sent him home to his mama.

Teacher. But Stephen wasn't one to take no for an answer.
What did he do?

Gail. He got around twenty thousand kids together and
told them to follow him to the Holy Land.

Teacher. How did they go?

Only ALEC's *hand is up now.*

Alec. Me—me—Mr. Finnerty.

Teacher. Alec.

Alec [rising, cocksure]. They marched across France to the
Port of Marseilles, 'cause Stephen promised the kids that
the ocean would open so they could all reach the Holy Land
with dry feet.

First Boy. That's phony. The ocean can't open.

Gail. I seen it. It did in *The Ten Commandments.*

Second Boy. That's trick photography, stoophead.

Teacher. Quiet. Then what happened, Alec?

Alec [*rising*]. The ocean didn't open, and these two ship-owners said they would ferry the kids to the Holy Land free of charge.

Teacher. Correct. Then all the children crowded into seven ships and sailed forth singing hymns of victory. Two of the ships were wrecked and all the children on board were drowned. The other children were carried to North Africa and either murdered or sold as slaves. [*He pauses and gazes at the children who are waiting breathlessly for him to continue.*] Why do you suppose Stephen wanted to lead this Crusade of children?

First Boy. He was kooked.

Second Boy. He was being paid by the pope to get up a gang to stomp the infidels.

Twilight. The infidels? Ain't they from 145th Street?

Gales of laughter. The TEACHER *raps on the desk.*

Teacher. Order. [*The children become silent.*] Alec.

Alec [*rising*]. Stephen had a vision.

Teacher. What do you mean by a vision, Alec?

Alec. That's something you see that's really not there. Like a ghost or a spook or something.

Teacher. Do you believe that, Alec?

Alec. No. There's no such thing as visions.

Teacher. Does anyone here believe something else? [*Slowly and timidly* MATTY's *hand goes up.*] Matty. You believe that Stephen had a real vision?

Matty [*rising slowly*]. Yes—I——

Teacher. What do you think a vision is?

Matty. It's God coming and telling you to do something.

Teacher. Do you believe in God?

Matty. Yes.

Teacher. And you believe Stephen had a vision just because he said so?

Matty [*in a low voice*]. Yes.

Teacher. Have you ever had a vision?

Matty [*stands awkwardly, as if he wants to sit*]. No.

Teacher. Do you know anyone who has?

Matty. Yes.

> *He suddenly realizes his mistake and starts to sit.*

Teacher. Don't sit. Who is this person? [MATTY *is unable to talk. He tries again to sit.*] Don't sit. I finally get you to speak in class and I don't want to break the spell. Now these visions of this person, are they good or bad visions?

Matty. Sometimes they're good and sometimes they're bad.

Teacher. You mean a good vision makes you do good things and a bad vision makes you do bad things.

Matty. Yes.

Teacher. Then God couldn't have been responsible for Stephen's vision. Look at the horrible fate the children met as a result of that vision. Do you agree? [MATTY *nods dumbly in the affirmative.*] Well, then, if the vision was not of God, then what was it? [MATTY *is silent and confused.*] Alec. You help him out.

Alec. He was just kooky.

Matty [*rising*]. Maybe God wanted the kids to die.

Teacher. You don't really believe that.

Matty. Maybe God wanted to prove something by having them die.

Teacher [*aggressively*]. Prove what?

Matty. Somethin' holy.

Teacher. What's holy about thousands of children dying horribly? [MATTY *is a little frightened by the* TEACHER's *reaction.*] Tell me, Mollusca. You believe in visions. Why have you never had one?

Matty. Because——

Teacher. That's not an answer.

Matty. Because it only happens to people who are very brave—very worthy.

Teacher. What about the rest of the children? Why did they go marching to their deaths? They didn't see any vision.

Matty. Because if you die for your faith, you go right to heaven.

Teacher. Ridiculous.

Matty. Maybe they died to prove their love?

The word brings laughter.

First Boy. Love? Jees.

Second Boy. Holy mackerel! Love!

Catcalls. The TEACHER *shouts.*

Teacher. Order! Order! [*Silence.*] Love of what?

Matty. Of Stephen—for bein' able to see the vision.

A bell rings to end the period. The class rises and starts to leave.

Teacher. Wait—one moment. Take your seats. [*The children sit.*] Mollusca. Would you die for love?

Matty. No.

Teacher. Why not?

Matty [*after a pause*]. I'm afraid to die.

Teacher [*after staring long and hard at* MATTY *for a moment*]. Class dismissed.

The children all rise noisily and gradually take their leave until only MATTY *and* ALEC *remain.*

Alec. You really believe all that jazz about visions and all?

Matty. I 'spose so.

Alec. What are you gonna be when you grow up?

Matty. A priest.

Alec. A priest? Holy mackerel. They don't even make any money.

Matty. I don't care. Wanna hear somethin'? [*Singing softly.*] Agnus Dei, qui tollis peccata mundi, dona nobis pacem.

Alec [*impressed*]. What's that?

Matty. Latin. I was in a choir once.

Alec. What's it mean?

Matty. How should I know? If I was a priest, I'd know.

Alec. And you could sit around and have visions all day.

Matty. I won't ever have a vision.

Alec. How come?

Matty. You can't ever have sinned.

Alec. Did you ever sin? [MATTY *looks away and is silent.*] What was it? You can tell me. I won't tell anyone—honest.

Matty. I can't tell. But I did once—and that ruins your chances forever.

Alec. A lot of those prophets and Bible big shots had some wild old times and it never stopped them from having visions all over the place.

Matty. You mean they sinned?

Alec. Sinned? Those guys invented the word.

Matty. And even though they sinned they still saw visions?

Alec. Sure.

Matty. Are you sure?

Alec. Sure I'm sure. I wouldn't wanna be a saint, though. Even if someone came to me and said, "Cushman, you can have all the visions you want," I'd turn 'em down flat. Saints always die young and they always suffer—and they burn 'em alive and torture them.

Matty. What are you gonna be, Alec?

Alec. My mother says I'm gonna be a doctor because I have a very high IQ. Bet I'm smarter than you in history.

Matty. I bet you are too, Alec. I guess you're the smartest kid I know.

Alec. I guess so too. My mother's gonna put me in a special school for geniuses. I belong to the Children's Book of the Month Club and my mother says that soon I'm gonna have my own encyclopedia.

Matty. Alec. You're gonna be a doctor. What's cancer?

Alec. It's a disease and there's no cure for it.

Matty. What's it look like?

Alec. Oh, all ways. Mostly green and pussy, though—like poison ivy.

Matty. Like poison ivy?

Alec. Yeah. And if you get it, you better make out your will.

Matty. If it looks like poison ivy, I bet someone with poison ivy could think they got cancer.

Alec. Sure. It happens every day.

Matty [*brightening*]. Alec, you must be the smartest kid ever.

Alec. I am.

Matty. Alec, what would you do if—say someone—say your mother—even your mother—was gonna hurt you?

Alec. Does your ma wallop you?

Matty. Who, me? Not me. Never!

Alec. So why are you asking?

Matty. For this guy.

Alec. Can't he ask for himself?

Matty. Well, see, he's kinda shy about it, I guess.

Alec. Tell him to tell his father.

Matty. His father's not around.

Alec. When you say "hurt real bad"—how bad is real bad?

Matty. Awful bad, I think, Alec.

Alec. Tell him to go to the cops.

Matty [*excited*]. The cops! I couldn't go to—the——

Alec [*suspicious*]. Hey. Who we talking about anyway?

Suddenly TWILIGHT *sticks his head into the room.*

Twilight. Anyone seen my crayons?

Matty. Hi ya, Twilight.

Alec. Hi ya, dirty ears.

Twilight [*to* ALEC]. Hi, fat teeth.

Alec [*to* TWILIGHT]. Hi, smelly ass.

Twilight. How you know my ass smells?

Alec. I smelled it today in class.

Twilight. That was Finnerty's—you had your nose up his again today. [*To* MATTY.] I leave my crayons here, Molusk?

Matty [*holding up the crayons*]. Here they are, Twilight. Right on your desk.

Twilight. Whew! If I'da lost them crayons, my ol' woman woulda browned me.

Alec [*bursting into laughter*]. Browned you? That's funny. Well, I'll see you men around the campus.

ALEC *leaves.* MATTY *and* TWILIGHT *are now alone together.*

Twilight. Man. I don't like that cat.

Matty. He's the smartest kid in school.

Twilight. Smart, my ass—and that's draggin' all the time. [*He starts to leave.*]

Matty. Play some stoop ball, Twilight?

Twilight. No, man. I gotta go home.

Matty. It's early.

Twilight. My ol' woman worries if I don't come right home from school. Thinks I'm kidnaped or somethin'.

Matty. There's no such thing as kidnapers.

Twilight. Oh, yeah? 'Member Sammy Lopez?

Matty. That's just a story.

Twilight. That was no story I seen them carry outta the basement of one-fifty-three in a basket.

Matty. It wasn't Sammy. His folks just moved, that's all.

Twilight. That's right. Moved and left him all alone. That's how come he got fricasseed by Faceless.

Matty [*shouting*]. That's just a fairy tale.

Twilight. You oughta know better'n that, man. He live in your building.

Matty. I never seen him.

Twilight. I did.

Matty [*aggressively*]. How could you? He only comes ou at night.

Twilight. I seen him goin' around once about sundown—hobblin' through the ol' lot 'tween Sedgwick and Burnsid; Pokin' aroun' in them ol' crates out there—his collar up way high tryin' to cover his face and all. It was gettin' dark and the way I seen him was kinda fuzzy. But I knowed it was him. I knowed it the minute I seen the limp.

Matty. How does he limp?

Twilight. Like that. [*He imitates.*] He got one peg leg—and you can hear it scrapin' along the gutter. [*He scrapes the board ruler across the floor.*] Whoosh it go. Whoosh. Whoosh. You hear that after dark, man—make tracks.

Matty. What happened?

Twilight. I seen him goin' through that ol' lot—goin' whoosh, whoosh. And when I moved to go—bam! He turns and look at me. And bam! Quick as that I lit out.

Matty. Did you see his face?

Twilight. Hell! If I seen that face would I be here to tell the story? Sammy seen his face and that's how come he got fricasseed.

Matty. If he's got a peg leg, how could he catch Sammy?

Twilight. Once he catch your eye, then you can't move no more. You paralyzed. [*Picking up his books.*] I gotta go, man.

Matty [*taking out his money*]. Don't go, Twilight. I'll buy you something if you don't go.

Twilight [*looking at the twenty dollars*]. Man! Where'd you get all that bread?

Matty. My mama gave it to me.

Twilight. For what?

Matty. For nothin'. She just likes to gimme things.

Twilight. Man, you lucky. All my ol' woman like to gimme is whacks up top my head.

Matty. If your mama did somethin' bad, would you turn her in to the police?

Twilight. Squeal to the fuzz on my ol' lady? Man, are you crazy? Maybe on my ol' man—but sure not my ol' lady.

Matty. What do the police do with sick people?

Twilight. What do you mean, sick? [MATTY *makes a gesture of insanity at his temple.*] Oh, you mean them kind. My aunt Hattie Robinson say they lock 'em up in the dark. They put 'em in an ice bath and hit 'em with rubber and tie 'em up in an iron suit and——

Matty [*truly upset*]. Why do they put them in an ice bath with an iron suit?

Twilight. Man. How should I know why them cats do what they do. Maybe it's 'cause they want 'em to rust to death.

Matty. My mother's makin' ginger candy tonight.

There is a rumble of thunder. MATTY *is trembling.*

Twilight. Man, whatsa matter with you?

Matty. I don't know.

Twilight. Sure. I understand. Sometimes I feel just that way too. Ol' Finnerty give you a case of the dismals, that's all. Go home to your ol' lady, Molusk. It's gettin' dark and that ginger candy's gonna be tastin' real fine. I gotta split. [*He starts to leave.*]

Matty. Wanna look through my glass? [*He holds out the magnifier.*]

Twilight. What all can you see with it?

Matty. Anything you want.

Twilight [*peering through the glass*]. Man, you crazy. I can't see jelly beans. [*He starts to leave again.*]

Matty [*going after him*]. I'll walk you, Twilight.

Twilight. Suit yourself, man.

They start off together.

Matty. You're right, Twilight. I'd never squeal to the fuzz on my mama, either.

Blackout.

SCENE VI

The lights go up again. MATTY *stands in the hallway of his apartment building. He knocks on a door.*

MATTY [*knocking*]. Juan—Madonna—Anyone home? Madonna?

An elderly orthodox RABBI *appears in the hall.*

Rabbi. Ah, the stargazer.

Matty. Hello, Rabbi Lichter.

Rabbi. Tell me. What's your favorite constellation?

Matty. Virgo.

Rabbi. The Virgin. She who was lifted to the heavens when sin on earth became too great. What did you learn in school today?

Matty. About Stephen and the Children's Crusade.

Rabbi. What did you learn about Stephen?

Matty. We learned that he was a liar and that he never saw a vision.

Rabbi. Really.

Matty. And that God punished him for running away from his mother—to the Crusades.

Rabbi. He had no choice. He was picked. The path was set for him long before he was born. The path is set for all of us.

Matty. How come God let all the children be killed?

Rabbi. He was preparing their way for a greater glory. A child's love is one of the strongest forces known to man. It is different from adult love. It asks nothing for itself. Its loyalty is so blind that it is pathetic. It kisses the hand that beats it. It is capable of acts of charity and sacrifice that go beyond anything we can know or understand. Do you see why the children followed Stephen? [MATTY *shrugs, confused.*] Because the children loved God. So they marched after Stephen to prove their love of God. They sang hymns. The Shekinah shined in their eyes. They did not even know that they were small.

Matty. And they were brave and worthy?

Rabbi. Very brave and very worthy. Learn a lesson from them. Learn to sacrifice. Then you will learn to love your fellow men.

Matty. Rabbis can have wives and kids, can't they?

Rabbi. Yes. Of course.

Matty. How come you don't?

Rabbi [*laughing*]. Fate did not decree.

Matty. Didn't you ever love anyone?

Rabbi [*angrily*]. It's not a rabbi's function to love anyone. He must love all of God's creatures. [*Softening.*] There was a girl once. Look at me, old wreck, and try to imagine—there was a girl once. I don't recall her name. [*Pauses, thinking.*] She used to come to my congregation when I was a young rabbi. Her mother was dead and she lived alone with her father—a cruel man who treated her brutally. I scarcely remember the details. Anyway, I used to speak with her, comfort her. In some ways, in many ways, I was quite fond of her. But as she grew close to me, I turned from her. Somehow I wasn't able. I didn't know how. [*He halts for a moment as if his words pain him. He looks tenderly at* MATTY *and takes the boy's face between his hands.*] I would have enjoyed having a boy like you, Matthew. Come to me always. I want so much to be your friend. [*Thunder rumbles and lights dim in the hall.*] The storm is here.

Matty. I'm goin' to my mother. So long, Rabbi. [*He starts up the stairs.*]

Rabbi. God love and protect you, child.

The RABBI *stares upward after* MATTY *as* VOICES *come from offstage.*

Voice. Yoo-hoo, Teenie.

Child's Voice. One minute, Ma.

Voice. Right now!

Child. Aw——

Voice. Tell Melvin, too. It's gonna come buckets.

Child. You gotta go up, Melvin. You gotta go up, Melvin.

Melvin. I ain't.

Child. You gotta, you gotta.

Melvin. I ain't, I ain't.

The RABBI *is still gazing upward as the stage blacks out.*

SCENE VII

The lights come up again in the Mollusca apartment. Mrs. Mollusca is humming and working at her stove. She pours milk into a saucer and calls to the cat.

MOTHER. Here, Liddle. Come and get your milk. Come now, like a good girl. [*She puts the saucer down.*] Matty'll be here any minute looking for candy. [*She fusses at the stove in a state of high excitement.*] Wait till he walks in that door and gets a whiff of ginger. [*She samples a little of the candy and laughs.*] Last time I made it, he ate so much it spoiled his stomach. He's such a delicate child. [*She walks around the apartment humming and straightening things. Then she sings.*]

Come home soon, my love,
Come home soon to me.
Come home soon, my baby——

[*Suddenly she stops before the mutilated suit hanging in tatters on the door. She stares at the suit.*] Just look at what that boy does to clothing. [*Moving to a drawer, she takes out a sewing box and sits down to mend the suit before* MATTY's *return. She tries to thread the needle.*] He deserves to be punished. He needs to be whipped. [*She becomes infuriated at her inability to thread the needle. Fiercely.*] Dominick, Dominick. How could you humiliate me like this? What went wrong? I wanted you to stay. Why couldn't you try to understand? Dominick! [*Calling into the empty room.*] You're gonna regret. Run off and leave me, will you. You're gonna regret. You're gonna regret. [*She stabs at the child's suit again with the scissors. Suddenly she stands. She holds the scissors up and looks at them in horror. It is for her a moment of clarity in which she understands what she wants to do with the scissors. She runs to the window, throwing it open. She is about to toss the scissors out, but as she raises her hand she is stopped almost in mid-air, as if someone were holding her hand, preventing her from getting rid of the scissors. She whines childishly.*] Help me. Someone help me. [*She runs to the mirror. Her hands claw at her face as she examines the blemishes.*] Don't let me die, dear God. I can't die. I've got a baby. I've got a baby.

As she collapses on the floor in front of the mirror the stage is blacked out again. The right-hand corner of the stage is bathed in deep light. The strange atonal music of the fantasy is heard again. The dancers appear behind the fan-blown diaphanous curtain.

The tall woman, dressed in red, lies supine in a glass coffin, upon the lid of which reclines the motionless form of a red dwarf. The smaller woman, dressed in white, is being pursued by two forms in white who wear masks. As they capture her, they pin her to the ground before the glass coffin. One of the figures throws up her skirts and moves before her.

The red dwarf now rises in dreamlike fashion from the coffin lid. He seems almost to rise out of the glass-encased figure in red. As the woman struggles in the grip of the two masked figures, the dwarf slithers his way toward her and lies belly down on top of her struggling form. Slowly her figure turns red beneath the lights, as the shadow figure of the spider hovers over the fantasy.

As the lights go up on the stage again, the MOTHER *lies on the floor beneath the mirror. She still clutches the suit to her bosom.*

Mother. Don't come, love. Oh, dear God. Don't come.

MATTY's *voice is heard from outside.*

Matty. Mama, Mama, I'm home.

Mother [*stands and scrambles to the stove, hiding the scissors behind her*]. In here, dear.

Matty [*bouncing in happily*]. I did it, I did it. I fought old Finnerty and Alec and—— [*Seeing his suit on the floor and sensing.*] I——

Mother. Guess what I made for you.

Matty [*backing off*]. Mama—I—Alec——

Mother. Guess what I made, or you have to pay the consequences. [*She moves toward him with the pan of candy in front of her and the scissors behind her.*] Smell it. Smell it. Ginger. Ginger candy, love.

Matty [*backing off*]. Guess what you have, Mama. It's not what you thought at all. I'll bet you never guess. Mama, Mama, it's not like grandmother. It's not that. It's only poison ivy. You're gonna be all right. Alec told me, and he's gonna be a doctor. Mama, Mama. Please don't.

Mother [*moving slowly toward him, holding both candy and scissors out before her, she starts to sob as her struggle materializes before us.*] Ginger love. Ginger baby. Starfish—— [*She holds the scissors above her head.*] Yes, mother. Yes, yes.

Curtain.

ACT TWO

SCENE I

Later the same day. A waterfront saloon near the Hudson River. The name of the place is Cokeyflo's, as the sign over the bar reads. Around the bar stand habitués of the saloon— sailors, teamsters, longshoremen, petty merchants, and beggars. A blind and crippled creature hobbles about the stage on crutches, holding pencils out to people. He wears a placard on his chest which reads "Help the helpless." He moves about the stage mumbling. Thunder and lightning have brought all of these people together this late afternoon in May. Outside it grows darker and darker; inside, there is laughter and high spirits. The storm has given all of these people a close sense of camaraderie. They feel for each other—something like survivors in a lifeboat. As the curtain goes up, there is a crack of thunder and the lights dim in Cokeyflo's. The noise and laughter increase. The blind and crippled BEGGAR *starts his wobbly circumnavigation of the bar, muttering.* CARBO the barkeep, speaks.*

CARBO. Let there be light.

There is laughter and raucous interplay. The lights flicker and go up.

First Man. And there was light.

Cheers and applause.

Second Man. Hey—see that, Jerry?

Third Man. Yeah. How'd you do that, Tommy?

Carbo. Magic. Black magic.

Fourth Man. He's got a button under the bar, stupid.

Second Man [*inebriated*]. Let there be a little booze in my glass, Carbo.

Carbo. Drop a little bread in the till, and there'll be a little booze in your glass.

41

The BEGGAR *mumbles incoherently and circles the bar. More thunder.*

Fourth Man. The old man is snorin'.

Second Man. Your ol' lady's whorin'.

Fourth Man. Say anything you like about my wife or my little girl, but say nothin' about my ol' lady. The ol' lady's sacred.

First Man. What's that mean—thunder in May?

Third Man. It means someone stepped on a prayin' mantis.

First Man. Farmer's Almanac says it means a rainy summer.

Fourth Man. What happens when you step on a prayin' mantis?

Second Man. It means the mantis ain't prayed hard enough.

Third Man. Thunder in May means things start growin'. It means life.

Thunder rumbles. Lights flicker, go off for a moment, and then come on again. There is excitement and laughter. The old BEGGAR *moves to a table where* DOM *sits with a woman in her middle thirties. She is what remains of an attractive woman who has spent her life at a variety of pitiless drudgeries. Her name is* LILA.

Lila. Can't we go now, Dominick?

Dom. It's wet out there. [*He looks away, ignoring her.*] Hey, Carbo. Two more.

They sit quietly as the BEGGAR *hovers over them for a moment.* CARBO *brings around two more whiskies as the sound of cheap rock 'n roll music is heard in the background.*

Lila. What are you thinking?

Dom. How bad I screwed things up.

Lila. Why do people always say things like that when it don't matter any more? Did you mean what you said about takin' me west?

Dom. For Chrissake, Lila.

Lila. Come on, Dominick. Level with me. I'm sittin' here with you four hours listening to the rain on the roof and the lushes guzzling at the bar. My suitcase with my life's possessions is sitting over there in the corner, and I'm waiting for the wagon train that's gonna take me west——

Dom. So?

Lila. So I know right now, as I'm sittin' here and talkin', that once again Lila Riker has missed the wagon train.

Dom. Hey, Carbo. Two more.

Lila. If that's for me, I don't want it.

Dom. All right. Hey, Carbo. Make that three more.

Lila. You're sittin' there lookin' at the clock. I know what you're thinkin'—and sayin' to yourself—"She's startin' supper now."

Dom. She ain't started supper in two years.

Lila. And you're thinkin' about the kid. What's he doin' now?

Dom. He's downstairs ringin' bells with the moron. Ringa-ding-ding-ding. [*He laughs.*]

Lila. And your heart aches. You know why? 'Cause you're not free and clear.

Dom. Oh, Jesus, Lila——

Lila. There's no sense kidding ourselves any longer, is there? We been seein' each other on and off now the last four years, right? And every time we're on the point of doing something like making a clean break, this happens. We fizzle in some fleabag booze-parlor.

Dom. So?

Lila. So I'll see you in the morning when they sweep us outta here. I'll go back to the cafeteria and beg Ramondo for my job back, and you'll go home to your wife and beg her for your bed back.

Dom. I got news for you, sweetheart. I ain't been any-where's near that bed for the past two years. I ain't never goin' back.

Lila. Maybe it's better you do, Dominick.

Dom [*thrusts his trembling hands out before her*]. Look at that and tell me it's better I do. Just look. Look! [*He turns away from her. The hot defiance having left him, he seems a man who is about to unravel.*] Two months ago, I hadda get rid of all the knives in the house. She was using them to carve her own face. This morning the cat come into the house missing a chunk of ear.

Lila. How do you know it was her?

Dom [*thumping his forehead furiously*]. I know. I know.

Lila. What does the doctor say?

Dom. He don't know what the hell it is. Thinks it may have something to do with when she had the kid.

Lila. Did she have a tough time?

DOM *rises and moves forward down center. Lights dim as he starts to talk. This is to be treated largely as duologue, with* LILA's *voice coming periodically out of the shadows to keep the duologue going.*

Dom. She carried ten months and three days. That's some kinda record or something. One night he finally came. She held on to him for thirteen hours before Borella could separate them. Maybe that's why they're so buddy-buddy today. It was almost like she didn't wanna give him up.

Lila [*from the shadows*]. Or didn't wanna have him.

Dom. That ain't true. No one wanted a kid more'n Rose.

Lila. What's he like, Dominick?

Dom. Quiet. Very quiet. Alone always. He's a queer little stick. He didn't talk till he was five.

Lila. He's shy. I like that in kids.

Dom. No. It's not shy. It's somethin' more. It's like he's scared all the time.

Lila. Scared of what?

Dom. Things—people. We got some guy in the building got his face shot off in the war. The kids got Matty believing that this guy goes around butchering kids. They gave this guy a basket full of medals for something he did in the Pacific.

Lila. I'd be a little upset to see a guy without a face, too.

Dom. Matty never even seen him. He's a strange kid. That don't mean he's dumb. He's real brainy. Rose says he got the mentality to be anything he wants. [*He laughs.*] She got this idea he's gonna be one of these guys—whatya call 'em— they look at the stars——

Lila. An astronomer.

Dom. Yeah, an astronomer. In high school Rose had a crush on some guy who was gonna be an astronomer. So she's makin' an astronomer outta the kid. Takes him to the planetarium to study the stars. She even bought him some kind of little telescope so he could look through—— [*Laughs.*] Once I told her he was usin' it to watch Stella Rizzo undressin' across the way. She busted the thing in a million pieces. [*Laughs again.*] I was lyin'. He wasn't doin' that at all. He thinks it's a sin.

Lila. How could you do a thing like that, Dominick?

Dom. I don't know. I was tryin' to get her goat and the only way I can touch her is through him. He's still got one of the lenses. Takes it around wherever he goes.

Lila. Is she good to him?

Dom. He's her little candy boy. I can't ever remember her layin' a rough hand on him except one night a couple of years ago. I came in the house and she—she was holding his head under water.

Lila. Are you tellin' stories, Dom?

Dom. No. No, it's true. I could never find out what she was doin'. She said she was punishing the kid. I says, "For what?" She says, "For a lot of things." It bothered me. So I asked the kid a few days later. He played it coy. Made believe he didn't understand, so I walloped him. Then he told me his mother was washing his hair. You know what was funny about that, Lila? He really believed she was washing his hair. Now I could see she wasn't washing his hair.

The BEGGAR *hobbles around their table, mumbling.*

Lila. You can have her committed just on the basis of that.

Dom. I don't want her committed.

Lila. Committing her would be the best thing—for everyone. For her—for us.

Dom. What about Matty?

Lila. He'd come with us—west.

Dom. He'd go nowhere with me.

Lila. With her gone, he'd have no choice. He'd have to go with you.

Dom. You don't know him. He's stubborn—the way only quiet people are stubborn.

Lila. You're his father.

Dom. I tried to be. But whenever I got to the point where I was breakin' through to him, Rose'd come along and queer it.

Lila. You could win now, Dominick, if you had her put away.

Dom. As long as she's around, the kid's got someone. So no institutions.

Lila. Doesn't it bother you she tried to drown him?

Dom. I never said she tried to drown him.

Lila. You've got a duty, Dominick.

Dom. I got no duty to some sick, twisted woman who thinks I'm dirt—and to some queer little stick who don't care if I live or die.

Lila. You oughta be ashamed.

Dom. Ashamed? Why? For telling the truth? You know what I say about duty, Lila? I say screw duty. It's always screwed me. [*He moves toward center stage where he stands alone in the light. There is no longer any pretense of duologue. This is monologue.*] You wanna know what made Rose sick? Duty. Duty to a selfish old witch who lived seventy-six years and cursed her daughter with her dyin' breath. "Marry the Italian, Rose, have his child, and I curse you." [*He laughs.*] She used to tell Rose she was gonna catch a disease from me. Well, Rose married the Italian—she had his kid, and she was cursed. Can you believe that? She was cursed. And the kid was cursed, and—— [*He turns away, unable to include himself among the cursed.*] I'm not superstitious, but something went wrong with us right after the ol' lady died. And it was doing her duty that made Rose sick. Her mother was rotting away with cancer. She had three operations in five years. First they cut out her stomach, then they whacked off a boob, then they cut out her bowels and stuck a rubber tube inside her hip. [*He laughs again.*]

It used to break me up. It'd make me think of a sprinkler——
[A *pause*.] The ol' lady would lay around all day. She'd get
herself all disgusting and then she'd holler for Rose. "Rose,
clean me up. Rose wash me. Carry out my slops. Stay up
with me all night and fan me, Rose." And Rose'd be Johnny-
on-the-spot. "Yes, Mama," she would say. "Yes, Mama. Yes,
I will—yes, yes." It used to make me sick. That's doin' your
duty. Right, Lila? And all the time she kept needlin' Rose.
"Marry the Italian and I curse you. Marry the Italian——"
Rose couldn't take it. Rose was always sensitive and high-
strung. Well, I got news for you. The only real thing Rose
ever did was to marry the Italian. One Sunday morning she
turned her back on the ol' witch and we got married. She
was back with the ol' woman that Sunday night. And we
were happy, Lila. We lived in the house with the ol' lady,
and we made love in the room right next to hers. And whenever I heard her moanin' in there or rattlin', I'd make that
old mattress sing all the louder. Then Rose'd get outta bed
and go to her. The day after Matty was born, the ol' lady
died. It was like she was waitin' around just long enough
to see so she could curse us some more. We buried her the
next day and two weeks later Rose took to bed. First fever,
then cramps, then that went away, and then came the
rash. A couple of funny little red pimples like you see on
young girls—and Rose got it into her head it was cancer.
Doctor said it was all upstairs with her—in the head. He said
it would pass, but it never did. Father Cappella came and
talked with her a few times. Nothin' helped. Then one night,
about two years ago, I wake up about two in the morning
and Rose is sittin' up in bed in the dark. She says to me,
"Get up, Dominick. Mother's here." I get up. I walk
around. I check the kid. Everything is all right. I come back
into the room, and Rose is still sittin' up in bed in the dark
—but now she's talkin'. "Yes, Mama," she says. "No, Mama.
I will, Mama. Yes. Yes, Mama"—just like they was havin'
their breakfast together. Now it's just like it always was with
them when the ol' lady was alive. Only now the ol' lady is
runnin' Rose's life from the grave. [*He returns to the table*

where LILA *is seated. Suddenly he slumps into his chair.*]
Poor Rose. My poor Rose. My Indiana Rose. God forgive
me, Lila. God help me.

The blind BEGGAR *moves around the stage mumbling. Suddenly there is a rumble of thunder, and the lights go out, leaving the stage in total blackness. There is excitement and laughter. People are enjoying the storm thoroughly.*

Voice. Hey, Carbo, where's that button of yours now?

Voice. Where's the old lightmaker now?

Voice. Hey, who's the air raid warden for this district?

Laughter. Someone starts to sing.

"When the lights go on again—all over the world,
    There'll be——"

Lights flicker and go up. There are more cheers, laughter, and applause.

Fifth Man. Hey! Someone hooked my drink!

Carbo. Your what?

Fifth Man. My drink, my drink. Someone hooked my shot while the lights were out. [*Suddenly an inebriated man starts to tiptoe out. The* FIFTH MAN *seizes him by the lapels.*] You miserable——

Second Man. Lay offa me. I ain't hooked no drink.

A crowd starts to form.

Third Man. He's lyin'. He hooked it. I seen him.

Suddenly MATTY *enters, unnoticed, and stands observing the action quietly.*

Second Man [*terrified*]. I ain't never. I ain't never.

Fifth Man. It's oozing down your chin, you sotty bastard. [*Pushes him roughly.*]

Carbo. Knock it off.

Fifth Man. He hooked my drink. I had a full shot in front of me when the lights went out.

Second Man. I didn't hook no drink, Carbo, honest.

Fifth Man. You sayin' I'm a liar? [*Lunges at him.*] I'll crack his skull.

Third Man [*laughing*]. Get him. Get him.

Carbo. Knock it off, I said. [*He pours another drink for each of them and thrusts the glasses at the combatants.*] Here—here. Lush it up.

Fifth Man [*to* SECOND MAN]. If I ever catch you trying that again—I don't care whose drink—I'll eat your eyes out.

MATTY *is still standing there, drenched.*

Dom. What are you doin' here? [*He crosses to the boy and kneels before him.*] It ain't your mother? Nothin's wrong with your mother? [MATTY *is silent and stares at the floor.*] Oh, listen, kid, you don't have to be scared. These guys were just horsin' around. [*Turning to the men at the bar, he laughs.*] Right, fellas? Your mama's okay? Right? [MATTY *nods yes.*] Okay.

Lila [*coming from across the bar*]. For Pete's sake, Dominick, don't you see he's wet?

Dom. Sure, sure. I see. [*He turns to* MATTY.] For a guy with brains you're pretty stupid. Don't you know enough to come in outta the rain?

Matty. I got caught.

Dom. Sure, sure. Caught. Say hello to Miss Riker.

MATTY *turns to her.*

Lila. You better get outta them clothes, honey. You're gonna catch your death.

She kneels and starts to unbutton MATTY's *shirt, but he ducks behind his father.*

Dom. When a woman wants to undress you, co-operate. [*He starts to propel* MATTY *across the room.*] Say hello to the boys, kid. [*There is noise and laughter as* MATTY's *father carries him to the table, followed by* LILA. *The three sit at the table.*] Hey, Carbo. You got some dry rags in the back the kid could slip into?

Carbo. I'll check.

Lila. And get him somethin' to drink.

Dom. Hey, Carbo. Also a Coke for the kid.

Lila. No Coke, stoop. Hey, Carbo, somethin' warm. Tea or soup or somethin'.

Carbo. There's a little minestrone stuck to the pot.

Dom. Well, scrape it out and heat it up.

Lila [*to* MATTY]. Take off those shoes, honey.

Matty. They're not wet.

Dom. Not wet? They're gurgling. Do like the lady tells you, kid.

MATTY *slowly removes his shoes.*

Lila. Your daddy's always talking about you, so I feel like an old acquaintance already. [*She waits for* MATTY *to respond.*]

Dom. Hey, someone's talkin' to you.

Lila. For Pete's sake, Dominick! What are you jumpin' down his throat for?

Dom. He's no dummy. He can talk.

Lila. Leave us alone for a few minutes.

DOM *gazes at each of them for a moment, then rises.*

Dom [*to* MATTY]. Try and don't embarrass me. [*He goes off to the bar.*]

Lila. You know, I had a little one. He was a lot like you. He had your hair, and the same sort of little nose, and——
[*Pause.*] That was so long ago. I sure hope you and I are gonna be real fast friends, Matty.

Matty [*aggressively*]. Are you my father's friend?

Lila [*taken aback by his tone*]. Why, sure. We're friends a long time.

Matty. How long?

Lila [*a bit confused*]. Oh, we go way back. Since school. We used to be in the same class——

Matty. I don't believe that. He's much older than you. You couldn't have been in the same class.

Lila [*now really confused*]. Well, what I meant was he was a couple of grades ahead of me. [MATTY *stares skeptically at her.*] Well, now, as I actually recall it, it wasn't in school we knew each other. We used to live in the same neighborhood.

Matty. What neighborhood?

Lila. Why, Morris Park. It was Morris Park.

Matty. My father never lived around Morris Park. He grew up in Jersey.

Lila [*flustered*]. Well, maybe it was—— [*Calling for help.*] Dominick. Dominick.

Dom [*returning with old clothes*]. Whatsa matter? [*He collars* MATTY.] Hey, what'd you do now?

Lila. Leave him alone, Dominick. He didn't do anything. I was just calling for those dry clothes. [*She takes the clothes from* DOM.] Here, honey, slip into these.

MATTY *takes the clothes awkwardly but doesn't move.*

Dom. Jesus Christ! What a pansy I hatched. Look, there ain't no place for you to change here.

Lila. Stand in front of him, Dominick. [*To* MATTY.] No one'll see you, honey. Change right behind your daddy.

Matty [*to* LILA]. You go.

Dom [*collaring* MATTY]. Whatsa matter with you?

Lila. Dom, leave him. [*To* MATTY.] I was just on my way to powder my chin.

Dom. Don't go, Lila. He ain't ashamed of no woman.

Lila. Dominick. Please do it my way. [*To* MATTY.] I'm going, honey.

She leaves the table. Father and son stare at each other.

Dom. I thought your mama taught you some manners. You hurt her feelings.

Matty. Well, she lied to me. She told you and her were in the same class at school, and that you lived in the same neighborhood together.

Dom [*laughs*]. And you didn't believe her? I'm proud of you. Whenever a woman tells you something, be skeptical. Here. Get in the corner. I'll stand in front of you. [MATTY *stands a little awkwardly again with the bundle of clothes.*] Get going.

Matty. I'm almost dry——

Dom. Get going. [*He propels* MATTY *into the corner. Reluctantly* MATTY *starts to slip out of his wet clothes.* DOM *stands in front of him, talking.*] Yes, sir. Follow a lion before you believe a woman. That's in the Bible, kiddo, and you better believe it.

Matty. What happened to her little boy?

Dom. Whose little—— Oh, Lila's. How'd you know about that?

Matty. She said she had a little boy once.

Dom. Just your age he'd have been if he lived.

Matty. Who killed him?

Dom [*stunned*]. Killed him? Where do you get your ideas anyway? No one killed him. Tide dragged him out at Jones Beach a couple of summers ago. He washed up about three weeks later. I went down to identify him. He didn't have no face left.

Matty [*coming out from behind* Dom, *dressed in a huge set of old army khakis that make him look like a midget clown*]. How could you know him if he didn't have no face left?

Dom. There are ways—clothes, teeth. So you knew just where you could find me, huh? I guess the Hudson River ain't exactly no Boulder Dam. But don't be fooled, kid. I'm goin' this time, and I ain't never comin' back.

Matty. What happened to his face?

Dom. Eaten away by fish and salt water and—— [Matty *sits trembling.*] Hey, whatsa matter? You still cold? [*Throws his jacket around* Matty.] Hey, Carbo. What's the story on the minestrone? You plantin' it?

Carbo. Hold your horses. I only got two hands.

Dom. Never mind. I'll get it myself. Wait here, kiddo.

Dom *dashes back into the kitchen, leaving* Matty *alone at the table. The blind* Beggar *now moves in front of* Matty *and stops.*

Beggar [*shakes a tin cup in front of* Matty, *who takes a coin out of his pocket and drops it in the cup*]. God bless you, brother. God bless you.

Dom *returns with a pot of soup, just as the* Beggar *is leaving.*

Dom. You givin' your money away to that guy?

Matty. He's blind.

Dom. Sure, sure. Get this under your belt. You'll stop shivering. [Matty *starts slowly to spoon the soup as* Dom *talks.*] Did your—a—mother happen to say anything about my going?

Matty. She said she was glad you were gone.

Dom [*disappointed*]. Oh. You don't think she might like it if—if I came back?

Matty. She said she hoped you'd never come back again.

Dom. O.K. O.K., kid. You got no worries. You don't have to whip me no more. I'm down. [*Looks away, trying to appear unhurt.*]

Matty. Is she gonna be all right again?

Dom. Sure. Sure.

Matty. Like she was before—I mean? Isn't she?

Dom. Sure, sure. Just 'cause she acts a little funny now and then don't mean she ain't basically all right. She's gonna be swell—and real soon.

Matty. Does she like me?

Dom [*stunned*]. Like you? She loves you, stupid.

Matty [*relieved*]. I can't wait for her to be well enough again so we can go up on the roof together and look at stars —and——

Dom [*suddenly elated*]. Hey. Name some stars.

Matty [*shrinking*]. No—no—I——

Dom [*calling to the crowd*]. Hey, everybody. Listen to this.

Matty. I can't.

Dom. Whatya mean you can't. I'm always blabbin' to these guys about my kid. You gonna make a jackass outta me now in front of everyone? [*The crowd rings around* MATTY. DOM *stands him up on a table.* MATTY *looks around, terrified.*] Go ahead. Just a couple.

Matty [*still terrified, but starting slowly*]. Cassiopeia, Andromeda——

Dom [*thrilled*]. Listen. Listen to that.

Third Man. Marvelous.

Fourth Man. Beautiful, beautiful.

Second Man [*still inebriated*]. The Big Dipper.

Dom. Shut up! Go on, baby. Give us a few more.

Matty. I can't remember.

Dom. Go ahead, go ahead.

Matty. Delta Argus, Canopus, Monoceros, Pleiades——

Dom [*excited*]. Yeah, yeah.

Matty. Castor and Pollux, Aldebaran, Procyon, Rigel, Canis Minor, Sirius, Musca—— [*He stops suddenly.*]

Dom. He knows more, he knows more. Go ahead, kid.

Matty. Delta Argus——

First Man. He said that one.

Dom. Shut up. Come on, baby. [MATTY *has more or less stopped. He looks around helplessly.*] Whatsa matter, kid?

Second Man. The Big Dipper. Whatsa matter with the Big Dipper?

Dom [*to the drunk*]. Will you shut up! Whatsa matter, kid?

Matty. I wanna go up on the roof with my mother.

First Man. Hey, name some more stars, kid.

Dom. No. He's finished now.

He lifts MATTY *off the table as the crowd returns to the bar.*

Third Man. Reminds me of my neighbor's kid. Memorized all the stops on the New York subway system. Local and express. He could give 'em to you backwards, forwards, and sideways. Delancy Street, Hester Street, West Fourth——

Fifth Man. That's what you call photographic genius.

Third Man. What photographic genius? The kid was a moron. Nineteen years old, he couldn't wipe himself.

Dom [*to* MATTY]. Hey, listen. You don't have no trouble, do you? [MATTY *remains silent.*] She hasn't tried to scare you or hurt you or anything like that—— [MATTY *spoons some soup into his mouth.*] Why'd you come here?

Matty. I was just passing, and I looked in, and I saw you and——

Dom. Be honest with me for once.

Matty. I wanted to see you.

Dom [*pleased and touched*]. You missed me a little, huh? I—I didn't mean that thing I said to you this morning—about not likin' you—'cause I do. Hell, you know I do. I mean—well—go on. Have some more soup.

Matty. I don't want any more.

Dom. No more soup? [MATTY *shakes his head.*] There's something . . . I been wanting to tell you for the longest time . . . but it's a hard thing to put into words—— [MATTY *looks at his father.*] Loyalty—loyalty, Matty, is a good trait. And pride is a good trait, too. You get me. But having too much of either can be pretty rough on a guy— and having too much of both—well, that's murder. You get what I'm trying to say? [MATTY *is quite confused.*] Well, maybe you got just a little too much of both. See? Living is the real important thing, Matty. And sometimes to live you gotta forget some of these good things like loyalty and pride. Oh, I don't mean you forget about 'em completely. You just let 'em slip your mind every now and then, get it? What I'm saying is that in life you gotta know how to take second best.

Matty. What's second best?

Dom. For you, kid, second best is me. Your mama's first best. I'm not saying that I could ever come to be to you what she is. But I am saying that no one would work harder or care more for you than I would. I—I'd like you to come away with Lila and me.

Matty [*rising*]. The rain's stopping——

Dom [*pushes* MATTY *gently back into his chair*]. I been thinking about you and me. Your mama's not my problem any more, but you still are. I got a duty to you.

Matty. I gotta go now.

Dom [*his voice rising*]. Being loyal to your mother and standing by her 'cause she's sick is fine. But you better get it through your skull that you got a life to live—and I'm not sure you got too much of a life to live if you stay with her. [MATTY *tries to go but* DOM *restrains him.*] Wait. Wait. I'm not finished. Lila—Miss Riker—there, is a wonderful person. She'd be like a new mama to you. And she likes you. I know she does. [*Takes* MATTY'S *hand.*] We'd really like to have you, Matty. [*Laughs nervously.*] I didn't know what I was sittin' here and waitin' for all this while, till you walked in. Then I knew. I can't make it alone out there, Matty. I gotta have something of my own to hold onto—to work for—or else I'm just nothing. Please, kid. I'm asking you please.

Matty. I better go now.

Dom [*shouting suddenly, infuriated*]. I'm offering you the only chance at life you got. Now don't throw it away. [MATTY *starts to go.* DOM *grabs him.*] Why do you have to go?

Matty. I gotta feed Liddle.

Dom [*stunned*]. Liddle? Liddle? Oh, Jesus.

> LILA *appears and moves quickly to the table.*

Lila. Dominick! Dominick!

Dom. Stay outta this, Lila. [*Turns back to* MATTY.] Is that why you came here? You wanted me to help feed your cat? [MATTY *stares downward.*] Why'd you come?

Matty. I don't know.

Dom. What do you want? [MATTY *is silent.*] What the hell do you want from me?

Matty [*holding back his tears*]. I want you to take me home.

Dom [*stunned*]. Take you home? You can damn well take yourself home.

Matty. I can't.

Dom. Whatya mean, you can't?

Matty. I can't, I can't.

Dom. Go home the same Goddamned way you got here.

Lila. Dom! For Pete's sake!

Dom. Didn't I offer him something decent? You heard it, Lila. You couldn't believe it before. Now you heard it with your own ears. Ain't it just what I said? Ain't it? [*Turns back to* MATTY.] Why can't you come with me?

Matty. I want to be with my mother.

Dom. Go home, then. Be with your mother. Rot with her. Die with her. [MATTY *starts to walk out slowly. Everyone in the bar observes this scene.*] Hey, where's that gelt I gave you this morning—the twenty?

Matty. I don't have it.

Dom [*lunges for the boy*]. Liar.

LILA *rushes forward.* DOM *pushes her roughly into the crowd. He continues to stalk the boy who now backs toward the door.*

Lila. Dominick! Don't!

Dom [*to* MATTY]. Gimme.

Matty. I don't have it.

Dom. Gimme.

DOM *seizes the boy roughly, goes through his pockets, and pulls out the bill.* MATTY *starts to fight with* DOM, *slapping helplessly into the air.*

Matty. It ain't yours. It ain't yours.

Dom. Oh, yeah? Whose is it?

Matty. It's my mother's. She gave it to me.

Dom [*stunned*]. She gave it to you? Jesus Christ. It runs in the family, don't it? [MATTY *runs at his father and bites his hand.* DOM *slaps him viciously across the face twice.*] That's for lying. And that's for biting.

Lila [*screaming and rushing at them*]. Dom, no!

The crowd rushes forward.

Carbo. Dominick—Dominick——

Dom [*in a rage, to* MATTY]. Go on, get outta here. Go ring bells with the moron. Go up on the roof and play "Ring Around the Starfish" with your ol' lady. [MATTY *backs toward the door.*] I hope she cuts you like she cut the cat this morning. Get the hell out! [MATTY *flees from the bar, still wearing the outsized khaki outfit.* DOM *turns to the crowd.*] I offered him something decent, didn't I? [*The crowd withdraws from him and goes slowly back to the bar.* DOM *holds up the twenty.*] Setups for everyone. My kid's buyin' the drinks. [*Walks to* LILA.] You saw for yourself, didn't you? Now I'm free and clear, Lila. Now I'm free and clear, Lila. Now I'm ready to go—— [LILA *stares at him. Slowly she walks to the corner where her bag sits. She puts on her raincoat, picks up her bag, and goes out.* DOM *calls after her.*] I don't need you either, Riker. [*The* BEGGAR *drifts by, muttering his chant.* DOM *seizes the* BEGGAR *roughly, whips off his dark glasses, and flings his crutch into the corner.*] How much you take from him? [*Grabs him roughly by the collar.*]

Beggar. Only a dime, Dom. Honest, just a dime.

DOM *goes into the* BEGGAR'S *cup and retrieves the dime. He runs to the door out of which* MATTY *has just fled, throws it open, and screams in the direction in which the boy has gone.*

DOM. Here's your dime, you poor little bastard. [*He flings the coin after* MATTY. *Thunder rumbles.* DOM *returns to the table he just left. He slumps into his chair and tosses off a remaining whisky. Then, in a tear-choked voice.*] I tried to help. You all seen that I tried.

Blackout.

SCENE II

The deserted stairway. Inside the Mollusca apartment, Rose Mollusca can be seen rocking in her chair. She is mending MATTY'S *mutilated suit and humming softly to herself. Suddenly, from out of the shadows on the stairway, steps* DOM. *Moving quickly to the door of the apartment, he pauses a moment, with his ear to the door, listening to the high, sweet, almost childish sound of his wife's humming. He knocks hesitantly, and at the same moment Mrs. Mollusca's rocking comes abruptly to a standstill.* DOM *knocks again, but still she does not answer. Rising slowly, she crosses to the door on tiptoe, and waits there breathlessly. Now the two stand with only the door between them, both waiting and anticipating each other's next move.*

DOM [*softly, in almost a whisper*]. Rose? [*She still doesn't answer, but a smile of satisfaction crosses her face.*] Rose, honey? Open up. [*Gently, almost apologetically.*] I know you're in there. [*He knocks again.*] Don't play games, honey. Please. [*Waiting.*] Rose? Just tell me if the kid's there—if he's all right.

Mother. He's all right.

Dom. Where is he?

Mother. Sleeping.

Dom. O.K. O.K. [*Pausing, not knowing what to do next.*] Rose, honey? Lemme in. I gotta talk to you.

Mother. Go away.

Dom. I wanna come home.

Mother. First you run out on us. Then you come crawling back. Well, don't expect the door to be wide open.

Dom. I made a mistake, Rose.

Mother. No decent, self-respecting man could've made a mistake like that.

Dom. I come back. Can't you forgive it?

Mother. No. I can't.

Dom. I wanna help you, Rose.

Mother. It's too late. No one can help me.

Dom. You're not sick. That's all in your head.

Mother [*flaring*]. Don't you dare say that.

Dom. O.K. O.K. You're sick. But you can get better. We'll go to the hospital. We'll get the best doctor——

Mother. I'm going to die like she did—alone. In the dark. In pain and dirt. Not a soul to help me go.

Dom. I love you, Rose.

Mother [*contemptuously*]. You're so full of lies, Dominick.

Dom. It's true, Rose. I love you. And I love him.

Mother. You never loved him. I love him. He's my baby. I carried him. I had him in me so long he tore my insides. That's what ruined me. The only one in the world loves that poor baby is me.

Dom. All right, all right. Maybe that's true. I don't know. But just let's all be together again. I'll show you how much I can love him—and you.

Mother [*softening*]. Poor Dominick. All I ever done is hurt you.

Dom. I'm willing to be hurt. [*Laughing nervously.*] Hurt me, Rose. Go ahead. I can stand all the hurt there is as long as I got my Rose and my Matty. [*He rests his head against the door.*] Don't take that all away from me, Rose.

Mother [*gently*]. It's no good, Dominick.

Dom. What should I do? Tell me what you want me to do.

Mother. Go away. Take him with you.

Dom [*confused*]. Don't play games with me, Rose. Please.

Mother. Take him away from me.

Dom. How could you say you love him and ask me to take him away?

Mother [*crying out suddenly*]. Did he tell you anything?

Dom. About what?

Mother. Oh, the poor stupid little thing.

Dom. I don't understand, Rose. Help me understand.

Mother. I'm sick. Take him away.

Dom. I tried. I tried to take him this morning. And this afternoon, too. It's no use, Rose. He won't go with me.

Mother. He's got to. You've got to.

Dom [*losing his temper*]. The only reason you say that to me is 'cause you know Goddamn well he'll never leave you.

Mother [*fiercely, impatiently*]. Go away, go away.

Dom. Rose? [*There is silence again.*] Rose? [*Still silence.*] Rose? [*Silence.*] I ain't got no place to go. [*He turns slowly to go, then stops, remembering. He withdraws a brightly wrapped package from his pocket. He unwraps it. It is a toy telescope. He goes back to the door and knocks again.*] Rose? [*Knocking.*] I got something for the kid, Rose. A present, sort of.

Mother. Leave it outside the door.

Dom. Someone might hook it. Rose? Please. It's important to me he gets it. [*Pause. Then slowly she unlatches the door, leaving its chain on so that the door opens wide enough for him to hand the toy in. As she takes the toy, he grips her hand. The toy slips to floor as the two stand clasping each other's hand.* DOM *makes one last try.*] Rose?

Mother [*whispering back*]. No.

DOM *turns and slowly leaves. The* MOTHER *falls to her knees, retrieving the toy, clasping it to her bosom and sobbing as the stage blacks out.*

SCENE III

Blackness for a few moments. Then a single light illuminates the stage. MATTY *staggers breathlessly into the center of that light. He still wears the outsized khaki outfit that makes him look pitiful and like a clown. A single door at the left corner of the stage suggests the tenement hallway.* MATTY *runs up to this door, pauses for a moment, and then knocks frantically on it.*

MRS. CUSHMAN. Yes?

Matty [breathless]. Can Alec come out to play?

Mrs. Cushman. Can Alec come out——? I should say not. Who are you?

Matty. Could I see Alec?

Mrs. Cushman. Alec's studying.

Matty. Can I come in?

Mrs. Cushman. No, you can't. [MATTY *tries to squirm past her. She blocks his way and cries out to her husband.*] Arthur! Arthur! Help!

A man's voice is heard from offstage.

Mr. Cushman. What is it, Ida?

MATTY *scurries off.*

Mrs. Cushman [running, hysterical]. It was awful. Some little hooligan looking for Alec. He tried to attack me.

Blackout.

SCENE IV

When the lights come up again, MATTY *is standing under the window of another tenement. This is where* TWILIGHT *lives.* MATTY *calls up to* TWILIGHT *in a terrified whisper. There is distant thunder and the sound of rain on the pavement.*

MATTY. Twilight. Twilight, it's me. Twilight. [*There is silence and the rain. Suddenly the sound of scraping is heard along the pavements.* MATTY *gazes downstage desperately.*] Twilight! Twilight—— [*The scraping sound becomes quite loud.*] Twilight—Faceless—Twilight—Faceless—Faceless——

The scraping is very loud. MATTY *flees. In the next instant the old blind* BEGGAR *of the bar scene appears, scraping his crutch along the pavement.*

Blackout.

SCENE V

The lights come up again on the cutaway that permits us to peer into several apartments of the tenement. A blowzy and voluptuous middle-aged woman walks out of one of the doors. She is in a bathrobe, and she is carrying a bag of garbage to the incinerator by the stairway. Suddenly she hears a humming. She moves to the stairway and peers up into the shadows at the top of the stairwell, where the humming seems to be coming from. This woman is STELLA *Rizzo.*

STELLA. Who's that? [*Still the humming.*] Who's there?
     Mother. Have you seen the baby?

STELLA *goes up the steps. Mrs. Mollusca is sitting on the steps above. She holds the toy telescope in her hand.*

     Stella. How long you been sittin' up there like that?
     Mother. Have you seen the little red baby?
     Stella. The little red what?
     Mother. My little red baby.
     Stella. Your little red—— You mean Matty?

Mother. My Matty's gone.

Stella. Hasn't he come home for supper?

Mother. The night is full of terror for little children.

Stella. Maybe he's with his father.

Mother. His father's dead.

Stella. Dead? Dominick? Oh, Mary, Mother of Jesus. [*Crossing herself.*] How? When?

Mother. Early this morning. Cancer of the colon. It was only a matter of time.

Stella [*deeply moved*]. Dead? Dominick? I just saw him a couple of days ago. He was laughing and talking. I had no idea. Oh, Jesus, Jesus.

Mother. Now I'm alone, and the baby's gone.

Stella. Have you tried downstairs by the Espositos?

Mother. I forbid him to go near those people.

Stella. He's friendly with the boy.

Mother. He knows he's not to go near that diseased child.

Stella. Why don't you call the police?

Mother [*aggressively*]. You think he's like his father—lazy, worthless.

Stella. I never thought that of poor Dominick. God rest his soul.

Mother. Matthew's got quality, breeding——

Stella. Sure he does. Look, you go upstairs, and I'll take a look around.

Mother. The night is full of terror for little children.

Stella. The rain probably held him up somewhere.

Mother. Who'll take care of him now that his father's gone?

Stella. Things'll be all right. You'll see. [*She guides the* MOTHER *upstairs.*]

Mother. If he should come to you first, don't turn him away. Keep him safe from danger.

Stella. Sure.

Mother. Save my baby. My little red baby.

Stella. Sure, honey, sure. Now go on. Do like I say.

Mother [*disappearing upstairs*]. The night is full of terror for little children.

STELLA *is still holding her bag of garbage. Slowly she walks to the incinerator. As she opens the door, she shrieks, drops the bag, and slams the door again. Then she pulls open the incinerator door cautiously and peers in.*

Stella. Come out of there. [*No one emerges.*] Come on out. I know you're in there. [MATTY *slowly comes out of the incinerator looking more bedraggled than ever.*] Is this your idea of a joke? Your poor mother is sitting up there half out of her mind with heartbreak and worry——

Matty. Can I look at the fish?

Stella [*stunned*]. The fish? Your mother's hysterical with worry and you wanna look at fish! How could you leave her alone at a time like this?

Matty. Can I come into your house?

Stella. Honey, hasn't anyone told you yet? [MATTY *looks at her, perplexed.*] Your father——?

Matty [*angrily*]. My father's gone away. He'll never come back.

Stella [*embracing him*]. Poor baby.

Matty. Please, can I see the fish? Please? Please?

Stella [*deeply touched*]. Sure. Sure, honey. We'll go look at the fish. [*She leads him in and closes the door behind them. In the next moment* AUGIE *steps out of the shadows and stares at the closed door of* STELLA's *apartment.* STELLA *and* MATTY *are now in the apartment. The cutaway permits us to see* AUGIE *kneeling and peeking through the keyhole on one side of the door and* MATTY *and* STELLA *on the other side.*] Now only for a few minutes, 'cause I'm expecting someone. [MATTY *runs to a little fish tank that sits, illuminated, on a parlor table. He places a chair in front of the table and is now glued to the tank.*] I bet they all know you by this time. They probably look up outta that tank and say, "There's that spooky little kid again."

Matty. What's that one called?

Stella. She's an angelfish.

Matty. Does that mean she's good?

Stella. She's anything but that.

Matty. Is she a bad angel?

Stella. All the angels of this world ain't exactly what they're cracked up to be, honey.

Matty. I bet you'd be a good mother. [*He holds his magnifier up to the fish tank.*]

Stella [*laughing, but flattered*]. You kiddin'? Not me. I'd be a real bomb. Takes too much to be a good mama. I don't have it.

Matty. Why is she a bad angel?

Stella. Who? Her? She's a bad girl. She ate up all her babies a couple of days ago.

Matty [*suddenly in a trembling rage*]. Why? Why'd she go and do a thing like that?

Stella [*taken aback*]. I don't know.

Matty [*clutching* STELLA]. Why'd she do that? Why?

Stella [*frightened*]. How should I know? I guess she got hungry. [MATTY *hits the fish tank, almost toppling it. It is caught just in time by* STELLA.] Hey, whatsa matter with you? You crazy? You almost——

Matty. Why'd she have to go and do a thing like that?

Stella. I don't know. I told you. Maybe the kids were ugly and smelled bad. Maybe it's 'cause she don't know who their old man is. How should I know? Look. You better go upstairs.

Matty. No—no.

Stella. How can you act this way on the very day your dear father——

Matty. I'm not goin' up there.

Stella. Well, you damned well are.

She starts to drag him to the door. MATTY *drops to his knees. He won't go.*

Matty. If you tried, you'd be a good mother. Wanna practice on me?

Stella. I don't wanna practice on no one.

She attempts to drag him again. MATTY *now coils his arms around* STELLA's *legs.*

Matty. "Starfish—starfish—hugging to a rock——"

Stella. Hey, let go. Let go. [*She struggles to free herself.*]

Matty. Along came a typhoon——

STELLA *pushes him off. He crumbles to the floor, trembling.*

Stella [*now going to* MATTY]. Honey. What is it? That story about the fish? I was only kiddin', sweetie. Honest. Angel loves her kids. Worships them. Sends them to Sunday school. Gives 'em lollipops. Honest.

STELLA *kneels down, and* MATTY *hugs her desperately.*

Matty. Be my mother. Don't be afraid. Try it. Try it.

Stella. You got a mother, honey. And she loves you. You should have seen her only a few minutes ago sitting out there on the steps, worried sick, just 'cause you weren't home. Come.

Matty [*pulling back again*]. No—no.

Stella. Everyone's father dies sooner or later. It's tough, I know.

Matty [*aggressively*]. My father's not dead. He's alive.

Stella. Sure, baby. Sure.

Matty. He's alive.

Stella. Come on. I'll take you upstairs to your mama, where you belong.

Matty. Hide me. Hide me. [*Footsteps are heard in the hall outside.* AUGIE, *who has witnessed the entire scene through the keyhole, bolts away as a hulking, bearish man comes up the steps and rings* STELLA's *doorbell.* MATTY *hides behind* STELLA, *terrified.*] Hide me, please.

STELLA *is torn between the bell and the child's dilemma, which she is only beginning to grasp. The bell rings again.*

Stella. Go inside and don't come out. Never mind what you hear out here. Just stay in there. I'll get rid of this guy fast.

She pushes MATTY *into another room and closes the door behind him. She goes to the front door and opens it. The man enters, smiling. He carries a bottle of whisky in a paper bag. This is* VITO Tussi.

Vito [*grabs her, kisses her, and palms her buttocks, at the same time attempting to lift her skirt, but she wriggles away*] Hi ya, Studgie baby.

Stella. Lay off, will you, Vito.

Vito [*laughing and starting to remove his trousers*]. Baby. I didn't come here to lay off.

Stella. Keep your pants on, Vito.

Vito. Keep my pants on? Hey, what is this? What's goin' on here?

STELLA *walks past* VITO *and opens the door to the bedroom. She leads* MATTY *out past the astonished* VITO. *She stops at the front door and kneels before the frightened child.*

Stella. Go upstairs now. Your mama loves you.

Gently she pushes him out the front door and slowly closes it on him as he gazes at her. VITO *is still staring at* STELLA, *wide-eyed.*

Vito. Aren't you ashamed of yourself?

Stella. Shut up.

Vito. Ain't you got no morality, Stella?

Stella. Stupid. I was just looking out for the kid. His old man died today.

Vito [*genuinely touched for a moment*]. Oh. Too bad for the little guy.

Stella. He was scared to go home. Scared to death of her.

Vito. Of who?

Stella. The mother. She's a real strange one. A few minutes ago she was sittin' out on the landing in a bathrobe talkin' about a—a little red baby—or something. I swear it'd give you goosebumps. She's taking his death hard, poor thing.

Vito. We all got our own sorrows, Studgo. Other people's I can do without.

Stella. Poor kid. He don't know what hit him yet. Can't believe his father's dead.

Vito. Yeah. It's rough on a kid that age.

Stella. And she's thinkin', now that poor Dominick's gone, she's gotta care for the kid. She don't like that.

Vito. Yeah, it's rough. Rough.

Stella. Kids know when they're not wanted. They can sense it. They feel miserable and so ashamed they can't even tell their best friends. They go and hide—in—in incinerators. I should've done something——

Vito. Now what the hell could you have done?

Stella [stopped by that question]. I don't know. But I should've at least tried to do something.

Vito. I'll tell you what you coulda done. Nothing. Zero. Goose egg. You showed good sense. It ain't your bag of oats, so you kept your nose out.

Stella. You don't think I could have helped him?

Vito. Yeah, sure. You'd be some big help.

Stella. I guess you're right.

Vito. Of course I'm right.

Stella. I'm a great one to be going around helping people.

Vito [amorous again]. Let others help themselves, Stella Bella. I'll help you. [*Embracing her.*]

Stella. No one ever helps anyone in this world, Vito. Alone you come and alone you go. No one boosts you either way. [Vito *continues to embrace her hotly.*] You know what he said to me, Vito? He said I'd make a good mother. Ain't that a laugh?

Vito [his hands palm her buttocks and raise her skirt]. You know what your trouble is, Studgo. You got a soft heart and a real soft, sweet ass. [*Laughs.*]

                                        Blackout.

SCENE VI

Lights come on again. Matty *is on the stairway on his way up to the Mollusca apartment. He seems to be struggling with the idea of going up. Suddenly he hears along the stairway the strange scraping sound he associates with the faceless man. He shrinks into the shadows. He is about to fly upstairs to his apartment when the door opens and the* Mother *herself comes out to the head of the stairs and peers down.* Matty *shrinks farther back into the shadows. She* calls.

MOTHER. Love, is that you?

She stands there for a moment, peering into the shadows, and then turns around and goes back into her apartment. MATTY comes out. The scraping commences again. It grows louder and louder and then stops suddenly. In the next instant, a figure with a grotesque mask leaps out of the shadows. MATTY shrieks and leaps back. In the next instant, AUGIE has whipped off his mask and stands laughing at
MATTY.

Augie. You oughta seen your face, chicken. [*Laughing, he scrapes a stick over the floor.*] Sounded like the real thing, huh? Hey, whatcha doin'? [MATTY *starts to go.* AUGIE *restrains him.*] Hey, I seen you in there with Rizzo. Huggin' and rubbin'. What's that thing you were doin'. Starfish— something—on a rock. Boy, you're some cool stuff. I gotta try that. [*Laughs.*]

Matty. I wasn't doin' anything wrong.

Augie. Who said it was wrong? It was beautiful. And I had you pegged faggot. Did you see her naked?

Matty. No. I never——

Augie. Come on. You seen her naked. What's it look like?

Matty. What's what look like?

Augie. Ah, come on. Don't gimme that sweet little boy stuff. [MATTY *tries to get by him.*] I'm gonna tell your ol' lady you was lookin' at Rizzo naked.

Matty. That's a lie.

Augie. So what? She'll believe me.

Matty. If you tell her that, I'll kill you.

Augie [*first stunned, then bursts into laughter*]. That's the way I like to hear you talk. Now let's see if you're a man of your word. [*Twists* MATTY'S *arm behind his back.*] Fight. Come on, fight. You were lookin' at Rizzo naked. [*He twists harder, but* MATTY *does not fight.*] Kiss my foot. [*Twists again.*]

Matty. I'll kill you if you tell. [*Still he does not struggle.*]

Augie. Kiss it.

MATTY *is forced to his knees. Still he does not obey* AUGIE'S
command.

Matty [*crying out in agony, but still not struggling*]. I'll kill you. I'll kill you.

Augie [*determined, but his courage faltering*]. Kiss it, stupid. Jesus. For Chrissake—kiss it.

Suddenly the RABBI *appears.*

Rabbi. Stop! [*He separates the boys.*] Henschel, protector of the small and defenseless.

Augie. Whatya say, Father Lichter? [*Laughs.*]

Rabbi [*points to* MATTY]. What were you doing to him?

Augie. He ran away from his old lady. I was just taking him home.

Rabbi. I see. A born law enforcer.

Augie. He better get upstairs to his ma.

Rabbi. Suppose you follow your own advice.

Augie. What about him? [*Points to* MATTY.]

Rabbi. I'll take care of him.

Augie [*reluctantly*]. Well, he better get home.

Rabbi. I'll see to it.

Augie [*to* MATTY]. We ain't finished yet, chicken. [*Looks at the* RABBI *defiantly and backs away.*] Jesus-killer. Jesus-killer. [*Crosses himself and ducks down the steps.*]

Rabbi [*sitting down on the steps*]. Did he hurt you? [MATTY *shakes his head.*] For every thousand Henschels in this world, there is one Matthew. The odds against you, my child, are a thousand to one. It's very late. Why aren't you upstairs, asleep?

Matty. I had to do something.

Rabbi. I see. And have you done it?

Matty. Yes.

Rabbi. Very well. Then go upstairs now. [MATTY *sits and does not move.*] Well, why don't you go? [MATTY *remains sitting.*] Is something wrong? [MATTY *turns to the wall, almost assuming his own position of punishment. The* RABBI *turns him gently around.*] What have you done? Tell me.

Matty [*facing the wall*]. I made my mother unhappy.

Rabbi. It is written, "A foolish child left to himself bringeth his mother to shame." What shame have you brought to your mother?

Matty. I don't know.

Rabbi. Only today you asked me how you could become worthy. What did I tell you?

Matty. Through love and—sacrifice.

Rabbi. Forsake not the law of thy mother. Sacrifice your own pleasures to make her happy. Honor her. Be obedient to her under all conditions. Didn't you understand?

Matty. Yes, Rabbi.

Rabbi. So—now you're afraid to take your punishment. Come. We'll go up together and straighten this out. [MATTY *pulls back again.*] The quicker we get it over, the better you'll feel.

Matty. Were they afraid to die, Rabbi?

Rabbi. Who?

Matty. The kids who followed Stephen on the Crusades.

Rabbi. No. They believed that this life was not important. That it was the next life that counted.

Matty. I'm afraid to die.

Rabbi. What a strange thing for a little boy to think about.

Matty. I'm afraid to die.

Rabbi. Do you have faith? Do you believe?

Matty. Yes.

Rabbi. Then you don't have to be afraid.

Matty [*almost crying out*]. I believe. But I'm still afraid.

Rabbi. Come. I'll take you to your mother.

He tries to take MATTY *by the hand, but the boy resists.*

Matty. I'm afraid of my mother.

Rabbi. Afraid of your mother—who loves you?

Matty. My mother hates me. She hates me.

Rabbi. I've heard your mother call you Starfish. [*Pausing for the boy's reaction.*] Did you know that the starfish is one of God's blessed animals. If you cut one up into thirteen pieces each one will grow into a whole new starfish.

Matty. Really?

Rabbi. Really. God must love the starfish to bless them with such miraculous power.

Matty. Why doesn't God love people that way?

Rabbi. He does. He does. You cannot kill anything worthy in a man. Decency, dignity, kindness, love. You can stamp them out here, and they spring up there. Understand? [MATTY *shrugs in confusion.*] Your mother loves you very much. She calls you Starfish because she sees that you are one of the blessed creatures. Don't fear her punishment. [*He stares at* MATTY.] All right? [MATTY *nods affirmatively.*] Good. Wait here. I'll go up and talk to her first. [*He starts up the stairs.*] You wait here. [*At the head of the stairway, the* RABBI *knocks at the Mollusca door. It is opened by the* MOTHER.] Mrs. Mollusca. I'm sorry to disturb you. Your little boy——

Mother. Is he dead?

She attempts to push past the RABBI.

Rabbi. No, no. Of course not.

Mother. He didn't come home from school today.

Rabbi. That's funny. I met him in the hall this afternoon after school. He was on his way up, he said.

Mother. Oh?

Rabbi. He's downstairs. [*The* MOTHER *tries to get past the* RABBI *again. He holds her.*] He's quite tired, and he appears to be a little upset about something.

Mother. His father's run off and left us today.

Rabbi. I had no idea. Then that would explain his fear.

Mother. Fear? He's got nothing to fear.

Rabbi. Of course not. There are agencies and charities——

Mother [*flaring*]. Charities? Do I look like a welfare case to you?

Rabbi. No, no. Of course not.

Mother [*almost in tears*]. I'll do better for him than his father ever—— Don't let them take him away from me.

Rabbi. No one is going to take him from you.

Mother. Take me to him.

Rabbi [*restraining her*]. Mrs. Mollusca, there is an old Hebrew proverb that goes, "If you must strike a child, do it with a shoestring." [*The* MOTHER *stares at the* RABBI.] He's waiting below. [*They descend the stairs together.*] Matthew. [*They confront* MATTY *at the bottom of the stairs. He stares at them in terror.*] Your mother forgives you. [*As they approach,* MATTY *bolts up the stairs and heads for the roof.*] Come back, come back! You won't be punished.

Mother. Love, come back. Please come back.

Suddenly AUGIE *appears.*

Augie. He's headin' for the roof. I'll get him for you, Mrs. Mollusca.

AUGIE *bolts after* MATTY. *He catches him at the top of the stairs. They scramble.* MATTY *fights back savagely. As they scramble, the bell heard in the first act jingles from below.*

Matty. Juan—Juan.

Augie. The moron can't help you, stupid. [*As* MATTY *struggles, his glass falls from his pocket.* AUGIE *snatches it.*] It's Christmas in May, ain't it? [*He pockets the glass.*]

Matty. Gimme it back. I'll give you anything.

Augie. You had your chance, smart guy.

The bells continue to jingle.

Matty. I'll go down the cellar with you.

Mother [*from below*]. Matthew, Matthew.

The RABBI *starts up the stairs.*

Augie. It's all right. I got him for you, Mrs. Mollusca. [*To* MATTY.] Now, chicken, you get your neck wrung.

Matty. Madonna. Madonna.

AUGIE *drags* MATTY *down the stairs by the collar. People open doors in the hall.*

Man. There are people trying to sleep around here!

Woman. What that kid needs is a good beatin'.

Augie [*dragging* MATTY *to the Mollusca apartment*]. I got him for you, Mrs. Mollusca.

Mother. Be careful. You'll hurt him.

Rabbi [*going toward* MATTY]. Matthew.

Matty [*screaming at the* RABBI]. You said you wanted to help me! You tricked me! Liar—cheater—cheater—liar.

AUGIE *pushes the struggling* MATTY *into the Mollusca apartment.*

Mother [*to people gathered in the hall*]. Forgive me, please. [*She enters the apartment and closes the door behind her.*]

STELLA *and* VITO, *among others, look at the* RABBI.

Stella. Oh, Christ. Did you see his eyes? Did you see his eyes?

The RABBI *now stands almost isolated. He stares up at the door of the Mollusca apartment.*

Rabbi. Where have I done wrong?

Curtain.

ACT THREE

SCENE I

The scene is now similar to the first scene of the play. MATTY *huddles in terror by the window sill in his room that same night. He cradles the cat and rocks it in his arms. The sound of heavy rain can be heard on the window pane. Thunder rumbles.*

MATTY. Don't cry, Liddle. Don't be scared. It's only thunder. [*Rocking and pointing up and out the window.*] Soon the sky'll clear, and we'll see all the stars. You can't see 'em now, but they're up there. So far, so cold, so alone. They all look crowded together, but each one is really a hundred million million miles from the other. [*Suddenly the* MOTHER's *high, sweet hum is heard from another part of the apartment.* MATTY *is up in an instant. He runs to the door and listens to the humming. Then he flies quickly to his bed, falling on his knees by the side of the bed. He now clasps his hands in prayer.*] Hail Mary, full of grace. Hail Mary, full of grace. Hail Mary, full of grace. I know I was bad. I know I sinned. But I can't die now. Holy Mother. I know you just won't let it. [*He rocks back and forth, listening to the humming.*] Hail Mary, full of grace. Hail Mary.

As MATTY *backs into a corner, his room is blacked out. A dim light now comes up on the outer room where the* MOTHER *sits in a rocker and slowly rocks herself. As she hums, she watches almost hypnotically as the rain streams down her window. The strange music that accompanies one of her fantasies starts. The lights dim. Only the* MOTHER's *silhouette can be seen in her rocking chair as the third fantasy is played in the right corner of the stage.*

75

The figure of the tall woman still lies encased in the glass coffin, which is now tilted up on its end. The figure of the shorter woman in the white robes now dances with the little red dwarf figure, who appears to be locked to her by means of invisible handcuffs. Throughout this dance the woman struggles to free herself from the dwarf. The more she struggles, the more she becomes entwined in his grasp. Their dance is performed entirely beneath the shadow of the large spider that hovers above them. Suddenly the door of the glass coffin swings open. The white-robed figure within laughs hysterically in pantomime. The figure of the dancing woman now goes full red under the lights. The woman in the glass case holds out a shears to the struggling dancer, who seizes them and starts to chop at the dwarf. The lights dim.

The lights go up again. The MOTHER *is standing on the other side of* MATTY's *bedroom door.* MATTY *is still backed into a corner. The* MOTHER *opens the door. In her hand she carries a hatchet. Slowly she crosses the room toward* MATTY. *Her arm goes up, and in the next instant the hatchet is on the way down. In a split second, the boy scurries away. The* MOTHER *flails the air with the hatchet.*

Mother. Yes, mother. Yes, I will. Yes. I hear you. Goddamn you, I'm coming. I hear you, yes. I will. Yes. Die—die. Why don't you die already! [*She flails the air insanely and drops the hatchet.* MATTY *picks it up and starts to back out of the room slowly. The* MOTHER *slowly follows him.*] Love, you can't go. You can't leave Mother. Not when she's dying. [*She answers herself.*] No, Mother. I won't. I promise, I won't. [*Her voice changes.*] It's your duty to stay. Keep me comfortable, love, in these last hours. [*She answers herself again.*] Yes, Mother. I will. I will. [*Once more the voice changes.*] Clean me. Sponge this filth. I can't bear the stink of me. [*She answers again.*] Yes, Mother. Yes. I'm coming. I'm coming. Damn you. Die already. Die now. Die! [MATTY *watches her closely as he backs out.*] Stay, love. Stay. Don't leave me. I can't die alone. Stay. Stay. [*She sings through her tears.*] "Starfish, starfish, hugging to a"—I won't leave you to this shame. [*She lunges for* MATTY. *He swings the hatchet at her and grazes her hip. As she shrieks in pain,* MATTY *flees the room. She follows him down the stairs and calls as she falls to her knees.*] It's not me, love. It's not me. It's grandmother. Don't you see, I've got no choice. I can't leave you to this shame. It's not me, love. I won't——

MATTY *crouches beneath her on the lower level of the stairway. Now he springs to the door of an apartment that has been left ajar. As the* MOTHER *starts to descend the stairway,* MATTY *ducks into the apartment. He slams the door behind him and finds himself plunged in darkness. For a long moment there is nothing but darkness and silence. Then slowly a figure emerges out of the shadows.*

Matty. Who's there? Who's—— [*Silence.*] I can't see. It's too dark. Am I dead now? [*Suddenly the figure moves toward* MATTY. *There is the sound of wood scraping over the floor— a familiar sound to the boy. He suddenly realizes. The figure comes between* MATTY *and the door of the apartment.* MATTY *cries out, covering his eyes with his hands.*] I didn't see your face, mister. Honest.

Faceless. I've heard your voice before. Below my window— with the others.

Matty [*almost hysterical—his eyes still covered with his hands*]. I don't want to die. Mister, please, I don't want to die.

Faceless. Why struggle? Life doesn't want you—doesn't need you.

Matty. Madonna! Madonna!

Faceless. You know what's waiting for you out there, coming from your filthy little corner of this bitch universe. Better die young. Give it up early.

Matty. Madonna! Madonna!

Faceless. There are no Madonnas here.

Matty. She is! She is!

Faceless. First God fails you. Then people fail you. Then hope fails you. Then you die.

Suddenly there is the sound of bells outside.

Matty [*his hands still over his eyes*]. Juan—Juan, help. [*The figure starts to lumber out of the shadows. There is the sound of the wooden leg dragged over the floor.*] No—no. No——

MATTY *tries to bolt for the door but is blocked by the man, who grabs him.* MATTY *struggles in his grip.*

Faceless. Look at my face. [*The faceless man emerges from the shadows, a light across this face of facelessness. It is a face in which the eyes are covered with flesh. There is only the slightest remains of a nose. The mouth is simply a hole. Prying* MATTY'S *hands away from his eyes, the man lifts the boy's face not ungently to his own.*] Open. Open. Now look. Look.

MATTY *whimpers. He gazes silently at the face. Suddenly the struggle leaves him. He is silent and continues to gaze at the faceless face.*

Matty. Is that all?

Faceless [*falling on his knees before* MATTY *and bringing his face up close to the boy's*]. Just a silly old joke with a toothless grin.

Matty. Is that all it ever was?

Faceless. I remember. First I had no face. Then I had no heart. [*He feels* MATTY'S *eyes with his finger tips.*] I can feel your heart through your eyes.

Matty. I can feel your heart through your finger tips.

Faceless. I have no heart. It doesn't beat.

Matty. It does. I can count the beats.

Faceless. You're lying.

Matty. I can. One, two, three, four—— [FACELESS *keeps his fingers on* MATTY'S *eyes.*] Five, six, seven——

Faceless. I think I—— [*He laughs.*] Yes, I felt it then. I felt it.

Matty. Eleven, twelve, thirteen——

The bells jingle from below.

Faceless. I felt my heart. Tell me again how it looks.

Matty. Not bad, mister, honest. You never killed anyone, did you?

The bells become more persistent.

Faceless. Where are you going?

Matty. To Madonna. [*He starts to leave.*]

Faceless. Will you come again?

Matty. No. I can't.

Faceless [*calling after him*]. Don't go, don't go. I lied. I lied to you.

Bells ring from below as MATTY *closes the door and leaves.*

Faceless. Oh, God, have you no pity?

MATTY *now stands in the deserted hallway. There is a long silence as he stands gazing at his own doorway. A strange calm seems to have overtaken him. Suddenly* AUGIE *bounces down the steps. He is surprised to see* MATTY. *Spitefully he whips out* MATTY'S *magnifying glass.*

Augie [*peering through the glass*]. I spy a little roach.

Matty. A magnifier makes things bigger.

Augie. Then this one's working backwards. How come your ol' lady let you out again?

Matty. I do what I please.

Augie. So do I. But that's 'cause my ol' lady don't care about what I please to do. [*He laughs.*] Your ol' lady's out of her skull.

Matty [*calmly*]. I know.

Augie [*surprised by* MATTY'S *reaction*]. Yeah? How come?

Matty. 'Cause she thinks she's dying, and she's not. And she's always talking to her mother like she was still alive. And 'cause—'cause——

Augie [*interested*]. Yeah?

Matty. Oh, lots of things.

Augie. She hates you, your ol' lady. I can tell.

Matty. I know.

Augie [*puzzled*]. Don't you care?

Matty. No.

Augie. I don't either. I used to. I mean when I first found out, it bugged me a little. You know, not wanting people to find out and all. Then one day I decided my ol' lady wasn't worth my carin' a Goddamn how she felt, and then I stopped carin'.

Matty. I don't care any more either.

Augie. You're better off, Chick. Believe me. [*He pats* MATTY *on the back affectionately. Then he looks at the magnifier.*] Hey, what's this thing good for, anyway?

Matty. You ever seen Vega of the Lyra?

Augie [*confused*]. Who?

Matty. Vega of the Lyra. It's a star. You can see it swell through that.

Augie. Yeah? Show me.

Matty. I can't. I gotta go somewhere.

Augie. Who you kiddin'? You ain't got no place to go. Come on. Teach me the stars.

Matty. I'm going to Madonna.

Augie. She won't open the door this time of night.

Matty. She asked me to come.

Augie. Come on down with me. I'll teach you how to live. [MATTY *goes to the door of* MADONNA'S *apartment. Bells tingle from behind it. Just as* MATTY *is about to ring,* AUGIE *springs and stays his hand.*] I said come with me.

Matty. No.

Augie. I'll drag you down there.

Matty. I'll yell so loud I'll have the whole house up. Then they'd call the police and I'd tell them what you did to Teddy Morello in the cellar—and then they'd lock you up.

Augie [*grabbing him*]. I'd split your skull.

Matty. So what?

Augie. Are you nuts?

Matty. I feel great. [*He turns back to the door of the apartment.*]

Augie. Hey. [MATTY *turns.*] Can I come with you?

Matty. No. Madonna don't like you.

Augie. Well, I don't like no Spicks either. And you can tell her that.

Matty. Hey, you want me to go down the cellar with you?

Augie. Yeah.

Matty. Then give me my glass back.

Augie. If I give you the glass back, you'll come down? [MATTY *nods.* AUGIE *thrusts the glass at him.*] Come on.

Matty. First I gotta see Juan.

Augie. No deal—no deal. [*He grabs the glass back.*]

Matty [*shrugging*]. O.K. No deal. [*He turns to* MADONNA'S *door.*]

Augie. How come you gotta take the glass in there?

Matty. 'Cause I promised.

Augie. If I give it to you, how do I know you'll keep your end of the deal?

Matty. I promise.

Augie. Big deal. What's that mean?

Matty. A promise is a promise.

Augie. Not where I come from.

Matty. Give me the glass and go down the cellar and wait. I'll be there as soon as I see Juan.

Augie. How long is that supposed to take?

Matty. A few minutes.

Augie. Then you'll come? [MATTY *nods and* AUGIE *responds uncertainly.*] You double-cross me, I'll split your skull.

AUGIE *throws the glass into* MATTY'S *hand and bolts down the steps. As* MATTY *holds the glass in his hand, he smiles for the first time in the play. Then, as bells jingle from within, he rings* MADONNA'S *doorbell.*

SCENE II

From inside the apartment we hear the jingle of the bells. They ring in regularly spaced intervals throughout this final scene. It is almost as if they toll. A darkly attractive Puerto Rican woman opens the door. She is dressed almost gypsy fashion. Around her neck she wears a large gold medallion of the Virgin.

MADONNA [*staring down at* MATTY]. *Dios. Que pase, ange-lito?*

Matty [*standing outside the door*]. I looked for you all day.

Madonna. It's late, *niño*. What's the matter?

Matty. I thought you went away. I thought you left me.

Madonna. No, no. I take him to visit his grandmother.

Matty. Can I see him, Madonna?

Madonna. It's late. He's tired.

Matty. Just for a little.

Madonna. What about your mama?

Matty. She says it's O.K. Please.

Madonna [*softening, she stands aside*]. *Seguro, angelito.* [*As he enters,* MADONNA *stares at the outsized outfit of khakis from Cokeyflo's. She laughs.*] *Que payaso.* Is it Halloween? [*The bell rings noisily from the next room.*] He knows you are here, *angelito.* [MADONNA *leads* MATTY *into an adjoining room. It is a room of shadows. A Mongoloid boy of inde-terminate age sits on the floor, playing with a small hand bell. Behind the child is a stained glass window of the Holy Mother staring down upon the child who plays on the floor.*] Hey, Johnny. Surprise for you. [*The Mongoloid coos happily when he sees* MATTY, *who now falls on the floor beside the moron. The moron feels* MATTY'S *face.*] He says he's in fine health and happy to see you, *niño.*

Matty. I know.

Madonna. Come. We all sit together and have a visit. [MADONNA *lifts the dead weight of* JUAN *and leads him to a chair that is placed before the stained glass window. A street lamp glows through the window, illuminating it.* JUAN *sits on his mother's lap, his long legs dangling over her knees.* MATTY *sits on the floor, his back to the audience, facing* MADONNA *and the moron.*] Johnny, let's show your friend what we learned today.

The moron coos happily as he and his mother start to recite in unison. The moron's speech should be just articulate enough to distinguish a word here and there.

Madonna and *Juan*. Now—I—lay me—down—to—sleep. I—pray—the—Lord—my soul—to—keep——

Matty [*joining the other two*]. If I die before I wake—I pray the Lord—my—soul to take.

Laughs, ad-libs, applause among the three.

Madonna. Now it's your turn, *niño*. Tell us a story.

Matty. I don't know any.

Madonna. What did you learn in school today? [MATTY *thinks and shrugs*.] *Fingido*. Sure you learned something.

Matty. I learned about the Children's Crusade.

Madonna. *Bueno*. Tell us about that.

Matty. You know about it, Madonna.

Madonna. How could I know, *angelito*? I'm stupid. Tell us.

Matty. No. I can't.

JUAN *rings the bell fretfully.*

Madonna. Now you make him sad. You have to tell.

Matty [*looking back and forth at mother and son, he stammers and then starts his story*]. A long, long time ago, there was a lot of sadness in the world. There was war and sickness and sorrow and people who didn't have no faith. There was a shepherd boy called Stephen who was bad and did so many bad things that his mama hated him and couldn't stand to have him around the house. One day he had a vision that the Holy Mother came to him and told him to lead this big Crusade of kids across the ocean to the Holy Land so people could have faith again.

Madonna. *Sí, bonito*.

Matty. And that he'd die there.

Madonna. Oh, no, *bonito*. The Holy Mother couldn't have said that.

Matty. She did. She said if Stephen died there, for the Lord, all his sins would be forgiven, and his mother wouldn't hate him no more. So he did it. He died there.

JUAN *tolls his bell and moans.*

Madonna. You make him sad, *niño*.

Matty. Don't be sad, Juan. Stephen wasn't scared to die. He was happy because he knew he'd meet his mama again in heaven and she would love him again the way she used to. They'd go up on the roof together and look at the stars and play "Starfish." Did you know that if you cut a starfish into a million pieces——

Madonna. What are you saying, *niño?*

                    JUAN *tolls bell.*

Matty. Nothin'. I—nothin'.

Madonna. What happened to the other little crusaders?

Matty. They were all drowned and beaten and killed.

Madonna. Why do you tell such a sad story?

Matty. It's not sad. It's happy. They were happy.

Madonna [*skeptical*]. Are you sure it happened this way, *niño?* [A *phone rings outside.*] Tell him something happy. I'll be right back.

She dashes from the room, leaving the two boys together. JUAN *has been upset by the story. He rocks back and forth, mumbling and ringing his bell.*

Juan. Now—I—lay me—sleep me—down me——

Matty. After tonight we'll never see each other again, Juan.

Juan [*rocking*]. Lay me—sleep me—

Matty. I don't wanna go. I'd much rather stay here with you and Madonna, but I can't.

Juan [*ringing bell*]. Sleep me—keep me——

Matty. All day long I been tryin' to figure out how I could keep from goin'. I thought and thought till my head got to pounding. And now that I know what to do, now that I got my mind set, I'm happy. Honest. I can't ever remember bein' so happy.

Juan. Happy me—happy me—— [*He rings the bell.*]

Matty. My mama's sick now. 'Cause of me she's been very unhappy, so I gotta do everything I can to make her happy. To make her love me the way Madonna loves you.

Juan [*rocking*]. Love me—love me——

Matty. I'm all she's got, see? And she's all I got. I can't live without her, so I might just as well die with her.

Juan [*rocking back and forth, ringing the bell*]. Die me—die me—die me.

Matty. I figured out today that it don't matter how long you live, just as long as you do good things with the time you got. It's not this life that counts, it's the next. I done some bad things, Juan, sinful things. [*He takes out his glass.*] I've used this to—to—look at—women—naked. And——

Juan. Die me—die me.

Matty. Don't say that, Juan.

Juan. Die me—die me—die me——

Matty [*offers his glass to* JUAN]. Look. Take this. It's a magnifyin' glass. [JUAN *reaches for it eagerly.*] Always hold it this way. [*He holds it up for* JUAN *to look through.*] So whatever you look at will be bigger and prettier than it really is. Never the other way. That makes things small and ugly.

Juan. Die me—die me——

Matty. In the summer, when the warm nights come, go up on the roof with Madonna and look at all the stars through the glass. They're hundreds and hundreds and hundreds of miles away from us, and the tiniest one of them is bigger than the biggest thing we got in the whole world. Bigger than the Empire State Buildin' even. And there are so many of them that you could never even hope to count them all even if you were goin' to live forever. [*He stops short on that word.*] Forever. Forever.

Juan [*now rocking more violently*]. Die me—die me.

Matty. Please stop saying that, Juan.

Juan. Die me—die me—die me—die me——

Suddenly MATTY *slaps him viciously. The moron howls out loud. In the next instant* MATTY *is hugging him. They rock back and forth in this embrace.*

Matty. Hit me, Juan. Hit me. Hit me back.

Juan. Die me—die me—die me—me——

MADONNA *comes rushing in.*

Madonna. What is it? What's the matter?

Matty [*still hugging* JUAN]. Hit me, Juan. Hit me. [MA-DONNA *separates the boys, dragging* MATTY *away from* JUAN *as he tries to go back to the moron.*] Tell him to hit me. I want him to hit me. I hate me.

Juan [*with a rocking motion*]. Die me—die me—die me——

Madonna [*leading* MATTY *out of the room*]. Leave him now. Leave him. Go.

She turns the light out in JUAN's *room, leaving the moron tolling his bell and sobbing softly to himself.*

Matty [*in the outer room*]. I hate me. I hate me. I hate me.

Madonna [*shaking him*]. What did you do to him?

Matty [*almost screaming*]. I hit him!

Madonna. You hit a sick creature? *Cobarde maricón.* How would you like it if I hit you? [*Raising her hand menacingly.*] Go away!

Matty. I love him.

Madonna [*contemptuously*]. You love him, so you hurt him.

Matty [*aggressively*]. Well, why should he be so lucky?

Madonna [*she laughs painfully*]. Him lucky? Fool! Go home.

Matty. You're the best person in the world, Madonna——

Madonna [*laughs contemptuously*]. Some day the good, holy people of this building will tell you all about me. You may not think I'm the best then.

Matty. I don't care what they say.

Madonna. What they say is true, *niño*—true. You think I am the best person. You want to know something about the best person? Sometimes she is ashamed to be seen with her own baby on the street because he is so—[*Turns away.*] ugly. Sometimes she wishes that he would die and that she would die with him, and then she is ashamed of what she wishes and ashamed of her shame, and then I want to take him and love him, and I want people to see me love him. [*She turns and walks away from* MATTY *as if she did not want him to see her face.*] The big joke, *niño*,—he doesn't even know who I am.

Matty. He knows, and he's happy.

Madonna. Do you think, *niño*, that Christ was happy to be nailed up? To be punished for our sins? Why should my Johnny be punished so bad for my sins?

Matty. He wasn't punished. He was blessed. He can see the Holy Mother.

Madonna. Are you talking coo-coo again, *chico?*

Matty. It's true. He sees her. My mother sees the Holy Mother, too.

Madonna [*sarcastically*]. And I suppose you too see her?

Matty. No. Not me.

Madonna. You are too hard on yourself, *niño*. You are the one who is blessed, not Johnny. You have been made perfect and beautiful. Eyes that see, a heart that feels. Learn not to suffer so much. It's not worth it. Go home. It's late, and your mama worries. [*The bell tinkles from within. They stare at each other. She senses something.*] Is something wrong, *angelito?* [MATTY *hangs his head.*] What's wrong? Tell me. [*She goes to him. He remains silent.*]

Matty. My grandmother.

Madonna. Your grandmother? *Demente.* You don't have no grandmother.

Matty. My grandmother lives with us.

Madonna. I think you are making fun with me, *niño.*

Matty. It's true.

Madonna. Then why do I never see her?

Matty. She never leaves the house. She stays in all day. She punishes me. She hurts me. She——

Madonna. *Embustero.* You come here tonight. You hit him. You tell me lies. I want you to go.

Suddenly, from outside, the high, sweet humming of the MOTHER *can be heard.*

Matty. That's her. That's my grandmother.

Madonna. *Dios mío.* Are you crazy? That's your mother. Your very own mother.

Matty [*quietly, with determination*]. No. That's my grandmother.

Madonna [*crossing herself*]. You frighten me. [MATTY *starts to leave the apartment.*] Where are you going?

Matty. Up.

Madonna. No, wait. Maybe you stay here tonight.

Matty [*starting to leave again*]. I gotta go.

Madonna. Stay, I said. [*She tries to stop him, and he ducks away. She speaks desperately.*] I don't understand you. I don't understand you.

Matty. I gotta go.

Madonna [*helplessly*]. All right. Then I take you.

Matty. No, I wanna go myself.

Madonna. Your grandmother may hurt you.

Matty. My mama won't let her. As long as my mama's there, she can't hurt me.

The bell tolls from within. MADONNA *kneels before the child.*

Madonna. Tell me true, *pobre.* What is wrong?

Matty. I don't know.

Madonna. For who are you crying?

Matty. For everybody.

Madonna [*wearily*]. All right. All right. [*Kissing him.*] Go to your mama, then, *niño.* It's dark and time for all the little crusaders to be safe asleep. Close your eyes, *angelito,* and tomorrow, when you wake, the storm will be over, the sun will be shining, birds singing on the windows and flowers blooming in the alley.

The bell tolls as MATTY *opens the hall door.*

Matty. Tell him I'm sorry.

Madonna. God blesses you, *niño.* You are his.

Matty. God bless you, Mama.

He snatches her hand and kisses it. He closes the door behind him and is once again on the stairway. He starts to climb to the Mollusca apartment. JUAN's *bell starts to toll urgently and continues with dirgelike regularity. The door of the Mollusca apartment is open at the head of the stairway. Suddenly* AUGIE's *voice is heard from the cellar.*

Augie. Hey, where dya think you're goin'?

Matty [*wearily, as he goes up slowly*]. To sleep.

Augie. No, you don't. [*The bell is tolling as* MATTY *continues climbing.*] You promised.

Matty. I never promise.

Augie [*shouting up from foot of the stairs.*] Liar! Cheater! You took my glass.

Matty. Living is taking. Good night, Augie.

Augie. Hey, don't go up there. She'll kill you. [MATTY *is at the top of the stairs. The bell is clanging from below.* AUGIE *sobs out.*] You saintly little son of a bitch. You don't deserve to live. [MATTY *crosses the threshold.* AUGIE *is sobbing for some reason he can't understand.*] Chicken. Gutless. Chicken. Bastard. Gutless. Chicken—chicken——

As the door closes behind MATTY, *the bells of the moron peel insanely.*

Curtain.

ABOUT THE AUTHOR

Herbert H. Lieberman was born in New Rochelle, New York, in 1933. He studied English literature at The City College of New York and did graduate work at Columbia University.

In 1960 he was selected to write for Albert McCleery's Television Workshop series, where he had *Christmas Song* produced.

In 1963 Mr. Lieberman won first prize in the Charles E. Sergel Drama Competition, which was conducted by the University of Chicago, for *Matty and the Moron and Madonna*.

DRAMABOOKS

MD 30 *Michel de Ghelderode: Seven Plays* Volume 2 (Red Magic, Hop,
Signor!, The Death of Doctor Faust, Christopher Columbus, A
Night of Pity, Piet Bouteille, Miss Jairus)
SD 1 *The Last Days of Lincoln* by Mark Van Doren
SD 2 *Oh Dad, Poor Dad, Mamma's Hung You in the Closet and I'm
Feelin' So Sad* by Arthur Kopit
SD 3 *The Chinese Wall* by Max Frisch
SD 4 *Billy Budd* by Louis O. Coxe and Robert Chapman
SD 5 *The Devils* by John Whiting
SD 6 *The Firebugs* by Max Frisch
SD 9 *Matty and the Moron and Madonna* by Herbert Lieberman

CRITICISM

D 1 *Shakespeare and the Elizabethans* by Henri Fluchère
D 2 *On Dramatic Method* by Harley Granville-Barker
D 3 *George Bernard Shaw* by G. K. Chesterton
D 4 *The Paradox of Acting* by Denis Diderot and *Masks or Faces?* by
William Archer
D 5 *The Scenic Art* by Henry James
D 6 *Preface to Hamlet* by Harley Granville-Barker
D 7 *Hazlitt on Theatre* edited by William Archer and Robert Lowe
D 8 *The Fervent Years* by Harold Clurman
D 9 *The Quintessence of Ibsenism* by Bernard Shaw
D 10 *Papers on Playmaking* edited by Brander Matthews
D 11 *Papers on Acting* edited by Brander Matthews
D 12 *The Theatre* by Stark Young
D 13 *Immortal Shadows* by Stark Young
D 14 *Shakespeare: A Survey* by E. K. Chambers
D 15 *The English Dramatic Critics* edited by James Agate
D 16 *Japanese Theatre* by Faubion Bowers
D 17 *Shaw's Dramatic Criticism* (1895-98) edited by John F. Matthews
D 18 *Shaw on Theatre* edited by E. J. West
D 19 *The Book of Job as a Greek Tragedy* by Horace Meyer Kallen
D 20 *Molière: The Man Seen Through the Plays* by Ramon Fernandez
D 21 *Greek Tragedy* by Gilbert Norwood
D 22 *Samuel Johnson on Shakespeare* edited by W. K. Wimsatt, Jr.
D 23 *The Poet in the Theatre* by Ronald Peacock
D 24 *Chekhov the Dramatist* by David Magarshack
D 25 *Theory and Technique of Playwriting* by John Howard Lawson
D 26 *The Art of the Theatre* by Henri Ghéon
D 27 *Aristotle's Poetics* with an Introduction by Francis Fergusson
D 28 *The Origin of the Theater* by Benjamin Hunningher
D 29 *Playwrights on Playwriting* by Toby Cole
D 30 *The Sense of Shakespeare's Sonnets* by Edward Hubler
D 31 *The Development of Shakespeare's Imagery* by Wolfgang Clemen
D 32 *Stanislavsky on the Art of the Stage* translated by David Magarshack
D 33 *Metatheatre: A New View of Dramatic Form* by Lionel Abel
D 34 *The Seven Ages of the Theatre* by Richard Southern
D 35 *The Death of Tragedy* by George Steiner
D 36 *Greek Comedy* by Gilbert Norwood
D 37 *Ibsen: Letters and Speeches* edited by Evert Sprinchorn
D 38 *The Testament of Samuel Beckett* by Josephine Jacobsen and Wil-
liam R. Mueller